Caring as Tenacity

Stories of Urban School Survival

UNDERSTANDING EDUCATION AND POLICY
William T. Pink and George W. Noblit
Series editors

Caring as Tenacity
Stories of Urban School Survival

edited by

Mary Anne Pitman
Debbie Zorn

University of Cincinnati

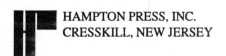

HAMPTON PRESS, INC.
CRESSKILL, NEW JERSEY

Printed in the United States of America

Library of Congress Cataloging-in-Publication Data

Caring as tenacity : stories of urban school survival / edited by Mary Anne
    Pitman, Debbie Zorn
        p. cm. -- (Understanding education and policy)
    Includes bibliographic references and index.
    ISBN 1-57273-210-5 -- ISBN 1-57273-211-3
    1. Education, urban--United States. 2. Socially handicapped children--
Services for--United States. 3. Mentoring in education--United States. I.
Pitman, Mary Anne. II. Zorn, Debbie. III. Series
LC5131.C35 1999
370'.9173'2--dc21   99-051612

Hampton Press, Inc.
23 Broadway
Cresskill, NJ 07626

Contents

Series Preface

Books in this series, *Understanding Education and Policy*, will present a variety of perspectives to better understand the aims, practices, content and contexts of schooling, and the meaning of these analyses for educational policy. Our primary intent is to redirect the language used, the voices included in the conversation, and the range of issues addressed in the current debate concerning schools and policy. In doing this, books in the series will explore the differential conceptions and experiences that surface when analysis includes racial, class, gender, ethnic, and other key differences. Such a perspective will span the social sciences (anthropology, history, philosophy, psychology, sociology, etc.), and research paradigms.

Books in the series will be grounded in the contextualized lives of the major actors in school (students, teachers, administrators, parents, policy makers, etc.) and address major theoretical issues. The challenge to authors is to fully explore life-in-schools, through the multiple lenses of various actors and within the contexts in which these actors and schools are situated. It is anticipated that such a range of empirically sound and theoretically challenging work will contribute to a fundamental and needed rethinking of the content, process and context for school reform.

It is now clear that one of the most compelling recent ideas in education has come from the work of feminists. In this volume, Pitman and Zorn have assembled a set of studies of difficult school and life contexts which show that caring is intertwined with power and desire. In difficult relationships and social contexts, caring must be tenacious. Tenacity is a force against the vulnerability of youth, and the disaffection of adulthood. Many feminists have been appropriately concerned that the emphasis on an ethic of caring has the consequence of justifying the traditional roles of women. *Caring as Tenacity* reframes caring, and links it to power and perseverance. For the authors in the volume, relationships that work in difficult situations require more than an ethic. They require diligence and determination. We welcome this book to the series. For us, it demonstrates the power of field work to reshape theory.

1

Caring as Tenacity: Stories of Urban School Survival An Introduction

Mary Anne Pitman
University of Cincinnati

This is a book of stories. They are mostly true stories. All of the stories were "discovered" during the process of conducting research—evaluation research, dissertation research, theory-driven research, and qualitative and ethnographic research. The editors were "involved" with each of the research projects, as consultants, advisors, principal investigators, and other related roles. We did not set out to study tenacity, or caring either, for that matter. We stumbled over it, or got hit in the head by its repeated presence.

I first noticed it, although, it was not yet named, when I was "taking a break" from a long stretch of research that wrestled with the conundrum of how it is that humans learn culture (Pitman, Eisikovits, & Dobbert, 1989). That research was conducted in the "naturally occurring" settings of hearth and home, of neighborhood and community, particularly with home schoolers, and not in institutional settings (Van Galen & Pitman, 1991). So, when the director of a small support program in a large urban school approached me with the request to conduct an evaluation of a mentoring program, I agreed.

Project HOPE had been serving as a pilot program in a citywide effort to establish mentoring relationships between area businesses and their personnel and urban schools and their clientele. Because the program's sponsors intended to extend the program to other settings, they were seeking evidence of the project's effectiveness in the lives of the Windham High School students who participated in it (approximately 150 of the 1,500 students enrolled). The HOPE staff, especially its director, was convinced that the program was indeed effective. Thus, the staff asked for an investigation of Project HOPE that would produce a description of how and where the project's activities existed within the in- and out-of-school lives of the participants, a descriptive narrative of the program's participants—kids, staff, mentors, teachers, parents, and others engaged in the activities and programs defined as Project HOPE.

The research team, which I headed, was very able to identify its own bias in the beginning. Mentoring was being touted by local business leaders as a kind of magical quick fix for the problems and challenges of urban schools. Never mind that these same businesses fail to employ urban adults, sabotage the kind of urban development that would provide equitable access to housing, and locate highly toxic plants within poor urban neighborhoods with large numbers of school-age children. In addition, the whole idea smacked of racism. Mentoring programs do not exist in the city's wealthiest suburbs or in its private schools.

Biases on mute, for the next 8 months, the team of three researchers spent approximately 10 hours a week interviewing, visiting, taking notes, reviewing records, and getting to know the staff (a secretary and two part time college admissions counselors), the students, the director, and the rhythm of their interactions. We learned that Project Hope was more than a mentoring program. It included tutoring, both getting help and giving it; career experiences; SAT/ACT preparation; admissions and financial aid counseling; seminars and workshops; a cable TV show; and a physical place to "hang out" during the school day.

When we sat down to try to make sense of our code list that included approximately 75 categories for more than 1,000 pages of field notes and interview summaries, we found that the program helped provide students with skills and experiences that contributed to student success in school and other settings. But what we were struck by was the significance of the relationships and interactions that arose in the context of these activities.

Our research revealed that HOPE functions primarily as a network of relationships based on caring, respect, and valuing. The decoration and design of the office facilitated this kind of relationship, and confirmed, most dramatically, that this space is not a regular classroom or office in the usual school sense. The office was a comfortable place for students. An old couch sat near the center of the room, inviting students to plop down and take a break from the pressures of urban schooling. A chess game sat on a table nearby, waiting to be used, and a computer was available loaded with their favorite games. The students had access to everything in the office—the typewriter, a computer, and the telephone. They frequently used the mirror contained inside the supplies cabinet to check their appearances between classes and at lunch time. They would stop by to use the stapler, grab a paper clip, or use the white-out to correct a paper. Students, staff members, and visitors may be offered food kept in a small refrigerator. If needed, there were certificates for food and bus tokens.

In short, the office was structured to provide physical and emotional sustenance for the students as well as to provide a space in which their voices and actions were recognized. And the students responded by coming to the office as often as their schedules allowed. The office was a haven for students, a place where they were trusted, and a place where they could be heard. Before school, students stopped by to sign up for seminars or other events, to seek information, or simply to say, "Hi." Some came looking for late passes. Some came because they were hungry and were looking for something to eat. On one occasion, a student came to seek help from the director because he had dropped out of school and decided that he wanted to return. The HOPE office offered comfort, conversation, diversion, and opportunity. The students shared their artwork, brought in pictures of their children, told stories and jokes, shared good news and bad.

The field of care extended beyond the office, beyond the school day, and beyond the job descriptions of the staff. Staff members had helped secure living situations for students with dangerous home lives, had helped students find jobs, made child-care and health care arrangements, and provided food and clothing.

Our report to the corporate sponsor concluded, therefore, that Project HOPE is successful because of the relationships it helps to establish and foster. We recommended that the environment and interactions of valuing and caring that characterize Project HOPE be extended to more and different members of the school population, and that it be replicated or integrated in the school program generally .

Curious about this phenomenon, for the next few months, in preparing a presentation of our findings at the anthropology meetings (Pitman & Samuels, 1991), we investigated the literature. With Noddings as our primary guide, we reached backward to such authors as Buber (1965), Heiddeger (1927/1962), and Montague (1970) to find some language to even talk about the phenomenon. From Heiddeger we borrowed a phrase that appears in our final report: They hear their names in "a field of care." But these theorists are all men, and, as masculinist philosophers they "should" on you a lot. So, we looked next in more familiar territory, feminist authors in the social sciences. We remembered and reviewed Bernard (1974), Chodorow (1978), and Gilligan (1982). They talk connectedness and interaction. That was certainly what we had observed. Next, we trained our attention on Noddings (1984), which some of us had owned, but never read carefully, and then to Witherall and Noddings (1991), Noddings (1992), and Martin (1992).

But, with the evaluation completed, and the presentation made, these voices moved to the periphery as we both got back to learning, focusing now on learning gender, (Harris, Pitman, Hensley, & Zorn, 1997), and, of necessity back to hearth and home, neighborhood and community. This turn was interrupted, again, this time, by the politics of higher education when the associate dean for research and development asked me, "Which ones of these program evaluations will you supervise/conduct?", and we both found ourselves back in urban secondary schools, this time in classrooms. Small vignettes from this series of studies are presented in chapter 7, "Holding On: Establishing Webs of Care and Connection," and chapter 8, "School with a Mission to Care."

This time we did not find a cozy office like that of Project HOPE. In fact, some of these classrooms, pull-out classes for young people 2 or more years behind their peers, were astonishingly bland, boring, and lacking in connections. We found some students making it, although many were not. Why? It began to be clear, looking at one setting after another, each of them very different in affect, that students who persisted and even succeeded had some kind of relationship that was tenacious. Somebody was hanging on, not letting go, not letting it go, not going away, harassing, reminding, asking, being vigilant, paying attention.

Zorn, having spent 13 years coordinating student support services targeted specifically for medical school students from minority and disadvantaged backgrounds, was cutting her teeth as a researcher-evaluator. Returning to classrooms in the urban district where she had taught several years earlier, she recognized something strangely familiar in some of these new intervention programs. She recognized a quality of relationship, the kind she had humbly attempted to establish with the medical students, or connect them with—relationships of tenuous trust and respect, sometimes over broad cultural divides, that would last 4 or more years and would need to involve an abiding belief and expectation that these students could indeed negotiate the sometimes threatening terrain of medical school culture. These relationships called on skills of cultural brokering between the often uncompromising world of medical education and the very different worlds of these students. She also knew that hers had been one in many such relationships involving family, friends, and numerous interested others that had contributed to each of these students' success throughout their schooling and was now supporting them in a highly competitive educational setting. By contrast, the students she found in the urban secondary schools had not survived schooling long enough to have developed the kinds of resilience she had admired in the medical students. Nor had they acquired their own personal support systems.

We have now come to believe that this kind of tenacious attention reflects an expectation built into the structure of elementary and secondary schooling. It is what the school culture means by "parental involvement." And for some students, making it through urban schools, it is a mother or grandmother who is the vigilant one. But it may be an administrator, a teacher, a custodian, an uncle, an employer, a case worker, a neighbor, a friend's mother, a friend.

Certain structural reforms taking place piecemeal in what Meier (1998) calls one-of-a kind schools seem to offer hope in that they point to the possibility of doing more than just expecting parents to be the tenacious ones, "to surround all young people with powerful adults who are in a position to act on their behalf in open and publicly responsible ways" (p. 359). These reforms take advantage of the enriched relationships made possible through innovations such as small learning communities within larger schools, vertical teaming, and especially, smaller schools, schools that are small enough, Meier continues, "for everyone to be known well by everyone else, and for schools and families to collaborate face-to-face over time. Small enough so that children belong to the same community as the adults in their lives instead of being abandoned to adult-less sub-cultures. Small enough to both feel safe and be safe." But, without systemic reforms that put real power in the hands of those who actually see and touch students, Meier says these one-of-a-kind schools rarely survive public scrutiny and expectations for "real" reforms in curriculum, instruction, and assessment. Such was the case with Kent, the school detailed in chapter 8.

So, we began to see these relationships in the subtext of all the studies represented in this book, all of them conducted for different purposes. The construct caring as tenacity was not part of the research design, the review of the literature, or the intentions of the researchers. Their data stories, however, make it so. And stories they are. We directed the authors to let the data speak. In some other forum, they can frame it with theoretical constructs, interpret it in light of related literature, or deconstruct it. Here we hope that readers will be as compelled to name the phenomenon as were we.

Data narratives have always been a part of standard field-based research. Their form may vary (VanMaanen, 1988), but without a narrative, there is no ethnography. Recently, narrative, as process and product, has joined other quantitative and qualitative research methods as its own, unique approach to understanding human phenomena. This was due, largely, to feminist methodology and its determination to "give voice" to women. "The feminist revision of the search for knowledge has sent us to new methods. . . . Women's personal narratives embody and reflect the reality of difference and complexity and . . . provide immediate, diverse, and rich sources for feminist revisions of knowledge" (Personal Narratives Group, 1989, p. 263). These same concerns motivated narrative research in education that, according to Casey (1995), proliferated throughout the 1980s. "The new narrative research has radically changed educational inquiry. The introduction of new information . . . has ruptured existing definitions and continues to change the very terms of discussion in education" (p. 239).

In this collection, we privilege story over any other form of data analysis. Why story? Story reveals context. The researcher cannot preselect variables and then limit the data to those categories. Instead, real lives are recounted as they are lived—in a richly contextualized social, ideological, and physical environment. In addition to revealing the complexity of context, stories allow the unexpected to emerge. Even in ethnographic and life history research, the researcher develops a structure for inquiry. Data narrative, stripped of researcher intrusion, privileges the voices of real teachers, and parents, and students, and others. Our willing suspension of our own categories for conducting research on the lives of those who inhabit urban school environments allowed us to recognize and, eventually, name the phenomenon of tenacity. Our insistence that the other contributors similarly suspend their own research questions and agendas facilitated this compelling account of struggle.

It is our belief that these data stories do confirm the major tenets of the construct of care as it is being developed in the educational literature. That literature has defined the components of caring as a concern with "relationship and commitment, mutuality and reciprocity, participation and continuity, concern for and acceptance of the other" (Chaskin & Rauner, 1995, p. 672). When the focus is within the schools, educational theorists prescribe that a caring school "must consider continuity of people and place . . . mutual trust and . . . a sense of belonging" (Noddings, 1995, p. 679). In his review of one of Noddings' books, Noblit (1993b), acknowledging that he has read widely in the feminist literature and the literature on caring, identified Noddings' "major new step in thought on caring—the notion of continuity being central to caring . . . [that] is more relational than interactional" (Noblit, 1993b, pp. 369-370).

For excellent reviews of the paradigm, we direct readers to the May 1995 special issue of the *Phi Delta Kappan.* and to two recent collections of studies that investigate caring and nurturance (Prilliman, Eaker, & Kendrick, 1994) and caring and justice (Eaker-Rich & Van Galen, 1996). We are pleased and humbled to join this conversation. We offer these stories of urban school survival with hope for us all.

2

"Oh No, Not My Child": One Parent's Refusal to Let Her Son Be "Pushed Out" or "Pushed Down"

Annie Hawkins
University of Cincinnati

This personal narrative relates the educational history of one African-American male from kindergarten through high school graduation as told by him and his mother, an educator and researcher. As part of the research team that looked at urban school dropout prevention classes (see chapter 7), Annie Hawkins was repeatedly struck by the fact the she was the dropout prevention device that her son used to get through urban schooling. Data analysis meetings were regularly interrupted by yet another story of giving up, or nearly giving up, as the researchers looked for who in the lives of the students was paying attention. Inevitably, Annie could relate a similar incident in her son's schooling. She knew, then, in a way she had not before, that she was the one paying attention, and again, and then again. Their story illustrates the value of constant vigilance as the educational institution presents a steady series of barriers to school survival.

This first data story also begins to hint at the paradoxical nature of tenacity as it exists, typically, in U.S. secondary schools. The school is neutral. School is a place you can go to—if you can get there. Once you're there, you can stay if you can figure out how to stay. The institutional gaze of schooling is decidedly inward, maintaining itself and tenaciously ignoring the lives of its inhabitants outside its bounds. Only this mother's persistent attention facilitated the possibility of her son's survival in the series of institutions that offered what they offered, period, no exceptions.

—Editors

School!! I never liked it and I never will. I actually do not hate school but I never enjoyed most of what took place there. During my early school years, up to grade 6, I had a pretty good time. My grades were not that great (I always made Cs and Ds), but I had fun with my friends.

From the time I entered school until I completed the eighth grade, I had three teachers who took steps to make every student in their classes believe that they were important and believe that they could do the work. They found ways to make learning interesting and fun and to help us discover things. These three, two women and one man, did not insult nor did they dismiss any of us when we did poorly. They encouraged us to try again. One thing that I always did was gauge my performance by the teacher's response to me and my friends. I tried hard when I was in the classes of these three teachers.

Another interesting thing about school was that I had only one male teacher between kindergarten and eighth grade. During my entire school career, I had only two African-American female teachers and no African-American male teachers.

I did enough to get by in most of my classes. I got through school because it was understood in our home that dropping out of school was not an option and because my parents continued to tell me that I could and would do well. I didn't get through school because school and the people in the schools were that interesting, motivating, or supportive. I know that school is important, but the process is often very painful for many of its participants. Some of my friends felt the same way that I did about school. It was because of the opportunities for social interactions that school was often bearable.

One of the happiest times of my life was the morning of graduation. I did not know for sure if I had made the June graduation list or the August list until I arrived at the school to line up for the march One thing that I did not want to do was to have to go to summer school after the 12th grade. As I marched around the field to take my seat, I spotted my parents in the bleachers and gave a victory signal to indicate to them that I had indeed made June graduation and the struggle was now over. In September following graduation, I began to attend a junior college but found more of the same as I had just experienced. I left at the end of the first quarter. Perhaps the future will find me deeply engrossed in study, but at the present, the world of work offers a refreshing repose.

Once upon a time, into a seemingly well-adjusted working-class family, in a large midwestern city located on one of the main in-land waterways of America, a little boy was born. There was absolutely nothing unusual about Scotty's birth. He was the second son born into his family, so we, his parents, believed that we knew exactly what to expect, because we already had one like him and things had worked out okay for the first one. His older brother was 3 years and 6 months older and his sister was 3 years and 8 months younger. Scotty was more laidback than his brother. He was a contented child and easy on the nerves, a real gently spirited child. The only event that was out of the ordinary in his early life was an illness that suddenly appeared when he was 22 months old.

Although a lot of kids get viruses during childhood, his illness was more than a virus and was never explained. Suddenly, one night he began to vomit. This was not unusual for a child this age, but within a few hours, he had lost all control of the muscles in his body and had become dehydrated. He was hospitalized and put into isolation on a ward in the local children's hospital. There, we discovered, were other children, all males, all under 24 months of age suffering from the same symptoms. The strange thing was that these kids were from all over the city, from all socioeconomic groups, and from a variety of ethnic groups. The only thing they had in common was their illness and the fact that they had not come into contact with one another before. There was never any mention of this mystery illness in the press, although by the end of the week, there were more than twenty kids on the ward.

I mention this because we revisited this illness time and time again as a possible explanation into the whys of his struggles during his school years. As parents, we examined every possible aspect of his existence when trying to justify, excuse, define, or resolve the obstacles to his classroom survival. Often, I knew that the school-based adults believed that I was an unrealistic parent who could not face the fact that I had an underachiever as a child; that my insistence on examining and re-examining learning styles, motivational techniques, and making modifications to requirements were just my way of denying the truth—that my son needed to be labeled for special education, and that I, as a special education teacher, could not face this reality.

On his second day of "real" school, my son cried as he was getting dressed. His request was that he be sent back to his other school. His other school was a nursery school that he had attended from April to July. These four months were his introduction to school and a transition from being home with mom and his new little sister to being at school with other children and adults. He loved the nursery school. In September, when he went to the new school, his hopes were high that there would be more of the same. Thus his tears. He did not cry the first morning because he did not know that things would be different. But the second morning his request was that he be allowed to go back to his other school, so that he could play. There is nothing out of the ordinary about a 5-year-old wanting to play. However, being a responsible parent, I had a heart-to-heart talk with him about growing up and being a big boy. I told him that school was not designed to be fun, it was designed to teach him and help him grow up. From that day until graduation day 13 years later, he seemed resigned not to enjoy school, although he did enjoy his friends and some of the things that school offered, like art, music, and sports. For him, the classroom held long hours of boredom, punishment, frustrations, anxiety, and failure.

Kindergarten was probably as interesting for me as for him. Kindergarten parents are often very competitive. I remember being in the class, helping out along with other mothers, when someone would point out that my son was not reading as well as her son. My response was that my son did not want to read and that I had confidence that just like potty training, he would learn it when he wanted and needed it. Kindergarten was where I became aware that he was not doing a lot of things important to school. He knew his colors, how to cut and paste, how to count, and how to play the games that interested him.

If he wanted something and didn't know where to get it or what it was called, he would ask his brother. His brother was always his spokesman. Scotty preferred to talk to his brother or sister and would talk to adults only if he had to. Throughout his school years, he preferred the conversation of his peers and never really seemed to enjoy talking to adults.

Kindergarten through Grade 3 settled into a pace that was relatively pleasant. He was in a special, individualized program that supposedly moved students along at their own pace. His elementary teachers felt that he was just a little immature, as boys tend to be, and that he would be fine. He was considered a sweet, courteous, obedient, cooperative child who would find his niche before too long and would blossom. His grandparents, babysitter, and family friends all concurred with those teachers. And so, hope sprang eternal in our hearts. As we observed him, we saw learning and mastery of many skills and we accepted the fact that he was not the student that his older brother was and possibly would never be because there was neither interest nor desire on his part to like schoolwork. He liked *going* to school, however, and did not try to skip. So, we accepted the appraisal that others gave of his educational powers and continued to encourage him.

The fourth grade brought a new school and a differing set of evaluations regarding his abilities, aptitudes, behaviors, and mastery. The K-3 program in which he had been enrolled had come to an end. It was an alternative program in one of the public primary schools and it ended at Grade 3. At this time, we decided to enroll him in the parochial school his brother had attended and in which his sister was now enrolled in the kindergarten program. This move was good because it simplified getting both him and his sister to school and to after-school babysitting. The school was three blocks from our home and the babysitter's house was next door to the school. The school's hours of operation also fit into our work schedules, so that I took the children to school and either one of us picked them up from the sitter.

At this new school, my son was often compared or contrasted to his brother, who was bubbly and outgoing. Scotty was quiet and seemingly introverted. His pace had always been slow and methodical, and the teachers in the primary grades allowed him to work at this natural pace. The individualized program of the lower grades made allowances for the individual differences. The fourth grade teacher, and those to come in Grades 5 through 8, did not make such allowances. He worked slowly and, because he hated being wrong, he would repeatedly erase and redo his work. Often, he did not complete his assignments in class, because he was striving to be accurate, neat, and perfect. It took him twice as long to do what everybody else did. The fact that he cared about how it looked was not important. Nobody cared how it looked if he never got to finish it. The pace at which he worked became part of the painful endurance of school for him and for me as the years passed.

Shortly into the first term at this school, it was recommended to us that we have our son tested. After posing some very direct questions as to why testing was recommended, and discovering that the recommendation was based on the fact that he was hard to motivate, the possibility of testing was rejected. Instead, we recommended classroom approaches that deviated from neat rows of silent children listening to an adult lecture. We suggested hands-on activities and discovery models. I, more than my husband, was viewed as intrusive and pushy. I could see dread as I approached the classroom, even on parent visitation night. As a teacher, I never wanted to take my classroom demeanor into my parenting role. But as a parent, I found that I could not propose, question, or offer assistance without it being construed as flaunting my credentials. I often felt that my son was given less of a chance because of me. Despite that, I was like a sentry—armed with my knowledge of him and his needs, prepared to defend his right to get whatever help and consideration I could find. I stayed on my self-appointed mission. It was my job to oversee his education or, I believed, he would get lost in the shuffle.

From grade four to grade five, it was as if he and I were going into battle every day. We were both exhausted when it came to dealing with the educational system. I came to understand why he hated school so much. He was powerless to get what he needed from school and I was powerless to get it for him. I was a force to be reckoned with and wanted to be taken seriously. All of us who teach know how to deal with the persistent pest of a parent. We smile sweetly, say the right things, never give them the ammunition to be used against us, and proceed to pass over the child. It happens often. I knew it was happening because I know the game. So school for him and for me was a continual game of taking turns with the professionals to get as much from them as we could and to get him to give as much as he would.

He seemed to weather well his C and D grades. They continued to dominate his report card through the intermediate years, despite our lectures to him on mediocrity not being acceptable. He attended a performing arts magnet school for 1 year, where he began performing and he enjoyed every minute of it. The distractions proved too costly, academically, because he put aside studying. The following year, as a seventh grader, after a great deal of serious discussion, he decided to return to the parochial school he had been attending since the fourth grade. It was worse than before. We spent a great deal of time conferring on how to assure success for him. He began to do his homework within minutes of getting home from school every day and stopped only to eat dinner. Following dinner he went back to his homework. Sometimes he kept this up until 11 p.m. There was no afternoon play time and no television. There was only the struggling to complete the assigned work. One evening I watched my son double over in pain, clutching his stomach as he struggled to complete and understand the work he was doing. Loss of privileges for failed tests due to incomplete work gave way to getting teachers to allow extra time to complete tests during lunch. When this took place, his grades went from failure to Cs or from Ds to Bs. Some teachers felt that it was unfair to other students to give Scotty more time to do the same things and so denied him the opportunity to succeed. One thing that was evident year after year was that he worked slowly and was too meticulous. He would erase his work to get it perfect, and therefore would not finish it. Most of his failure from Grades 4 through 12 resulted from this tendency. Many solutions were sought and many modifications in requirements were made. At one point, the amount of homework required from him was cut in half so that he could finish it without spending the entire evening doing so.

The amazing thing was the moment that he left the environment of the classroom, he emerged as the leader of the group. He was the student voted year after year in Grades 4 through 8, as the one person who everyone wanted to be their best friend. Several of his teachers told me that they watched him on the playground and that it was like looking at two different children. In the class, he was quiet and reluctant and on the playground he took charge and was decisive. Although these differences were observed, noted, and commented on, few of the teachers ever attempted to channel his playground strengths into the class setting. Once again, it was his fault that the shifts were not made and his playground behaviors were pointed out as justification for labeling him lazy and unwilling to try, unless he wanted to. He graduated from the eighth grade at St. Ars and prepared for high school. So far, he had managed to complete each year on time without repeating any grades. At this point in his education both of us— my son and I—breathed a sigh of relief. These four grades had been exhausting, both mentally and emotionally, for the two of us.

Three of our friends are psychologists and each of them encouraged us throughout the years to disregard the question posed to us about testing him. At various times during my son's education, I spent a great deal of time with each of them discussing him, his school performance, and what the educators who were dealing with him had to say. Each and every time I was told to forget testing him. There was no good reason to do so. So the answer to the question that was asked of us repeatedly, "Have you considered having him tested?" was yes, a thousand times yes, we had thought of it, but had we done it? No, we had not!

High school posed a different set of challenges. The things that he was very good at were off limits to him because of the deficiencies in his academics. He qualified for both the football and basketball teams, but was unable to play because of his grades. He attended summer school at he end of his freshman year because he failed English. Money earned by mowing lawns was used to pay for summer school. At the end of his sophomore year, he had to pay for two courses in summer school and the decision was made to leave the parochial school system and attend a public high school.

His junior year he enrolled in a commercial art program, and for the first time in his educational history he made grades that qualified him to be on the honor roll. The first two quarters of the junior year he made B honor roll. He had finally found something that motivated him to rise above his frustrations. He had also finally met an educator who was able to motivate him to excellence and encourage him to believe in his own ability to succeed. She was able to do this through simply expecting the best from him. This was the first time we were aware that he was gifted in art. His brother is an artist and we always thought that Scotty was merely mimicking what his brother was doing. Although he had always gotten his best grades in physical education, music, and art, there had been so much attention always given to the things that were not being done well, that those things that were done well received very little attention from us and therefore very little support and encouragement.

The junior year was a positive turning point in his life as far as education was concerned. The senior year was less spectacular. He had proven to his family and to himself that he could do well and now settled back to the cruise level to which he had grown accustomed throughout his education. The one thing that he decided during his last quarter of school was to be tested. He made the request because he wanted to know if there truly was some unidentified reason why school had always been a struggle for him. After a battery of tests, he was informed that there were no reasons for his concern. He was average in ability and intellect, above average in the areas relating to art, and could do well at his chosen field. He was given insights into how to maximize his study styles so that mastery of content material would come easier for him. He had been encouraged during the last 2 years of his schooling to trust his own creativity and to draw the pictures that he saw in his head.

The test results had a positive impact. I say this because, throughout my son's 13 years of schooling, he and I both went to school. I felt deep inside of me, the criticisms, the low expectations, the impatience, the transfer of responsibility for what was not learned, and the frustration of not knowing how to motivate him to excellence. I saw on the faces of some adults through the years, the determination to convince both me and my child that it was his fault that he had not understood some abstract concept. There were numerous instances in which the problems presented were not viewed by the educators as being related to methods, materials, or techniques, but existing in the child. In my opinion, it became a stance, we the school blame you the student for what you do not know and have not been able to learn. So many times during the years from fourth through twelfth grades, I was simply worn out. I did not want to talk to the teachers, see the midterm interim reports, or sign the report cards. But talk, see, and sign I did! For if we, his parents, did not persevere, then there was no way for our son to stay afloat. I had such strong negative feelings for what the learning environment did to my son.

Being a special educator, I am aware of the devastation that labels sometimes have and the mixed messages people get when interpreting what the labels mean. I was not eager to have my son struggle under the burden of a label just to eliminate a teacher's concern for situations that I believed could be better treated through other methods. Once out of middle school, there were no more inquiries into testing and labeling.

I recalled that as Scotty and his siblings were growing up, we would often discuss what each wanted to do and be when they got older. Scotty consistently stated that when he got big enough, he was going to drop out of school. This declaration was always met with my telling him that in this family, dropping out of high school was not a possibility. By the time he was in the eighth grade he would declare that, although he did not like school at all, he was going to graduate from high school. That was quite a commitment considering the struggle he was enduring at the time.

Our whole family was impacted by the struggles and frustrations that Scotty faced in school. As he worked at managing his time and energy, so did I. When he went to school, I felt that I went to school and when he graduated, I felt that we both deserved diplomas. Together we did what we had to do and the end was justification of the means.

3

Teen Mothers and Young Grandmothers[1]

Lanthan D. Camblin
University of Cincinnati

Patricia H. White
The Summit Country Day School

Lanthan Camblin, a developmental psychologist, has been investigating the developmental challenges involved with being both young and a grandmother for some time. In this study conducted with Patricia White, Camblin was assisting a local social service agency with needs assessment. At our urging, they took another look, turning their gaze away from what was needed (i.e., missing) and toward what was there. What they found were young women who were vigilant, doggedly attentive, not to the new baby, but to their own daughters, the new moms.

Here, again, we see the attentive behavior that has been institutionally labeled *parental involvement*. And it may be enough for some of the adolescent mothers. But one suspects that for most, it will not. These are not professionals, like Annie Hawkins, Scotty's mother in chapter 2, but poor urban citizens. Their attentiveness will be no match for schooling's even greater determination to ignore the chaotic lives of their clients, remaining tenaciously neutral toward the outside world.

—Editors

* * *

I remember the night she told me, I cried and cried. It wasn't what I wanted. I had dreamed all my life that MY children would go to college, that MY chil-

---

[1]The names of the respondents and their reactions were coded and confidentiality was strictly maintained.

dren would break the cycle and get out of this neighborhood. I did everything I could just so this wouldn't happen. When Alisa was a little girl I talked to her all the time about how important education was—I even got on a bus and rode up to a college and I showed her where I wanted her to go to school someday. We would always talk about her grades. . . . She was a real good student, teachers told me how intelligent she was. She brought books home from the library. . . . Even my mama told her how she needed school. You know, now I guess I was dreaming, but I didn't think so then. I thought my own mama didn't stress school enough and I was going to do a better job than she did. My mama told me to get good grades; she always told me how smart I was. I wish I had listened to my mama; I wanted so much to get out of the projects so that this wouldn't happen to my children. Just last night, it was so hot, I was sittin' outside thinking about how much I love Alisa's little boy, but I was wonderin' what can I do so this doesn't happen to my other kids.

This 30-year-old grandmother, Cleo,[2] went on to say that she had gotten pregnant at 14. Her mother took care of the baby. When she got pregnant again at 16, Cleo quit school.

I'm so scared right now. I take care of Alisa's son—Jamal. I want her life to be different from mine. I brought my children up going to church every Sunday. I walk them past the places where my friends used to live and tell them about the nice houses that they live in now. I tell them they got their houses 'cause they got their education, I don't want Alisa to quit school like I did. I make her do her lessons every night. She still sees Jamal's father— that scares me. I gave up on me. I gave up on me going to college; even today I want to get my GED. Some days I don't think I will ever move away from here. I talk to my minister's wife. She tells me to pray and to keep the kids going to church and it will help the younger ones. I am going to do everything I knows to keep Alisa in school. I need to make her stay in school. Alisa doesn't understand.

Cleo is one of the growing population of young grandmothers in U.S. society. These grandmothers know that their own lives will be forever altered because of a teenage daughter's pregnancy. Many of the young grandmothers remember the stress they caused their own mothers with the occurrence of an early pregnancy. The phenomenon of the young grandmother is not uncommon with the high rate of adolescent pregnancy currently existing in our society. In the United States, the typical age for becoming a grandmother is around 49 to 51, with 51 to 53 being the typical age for becoming a grandfather. Yet, the reality is that with changing demographic patterns, grandparenthood is no longer predominantly an old-age event, but is commonplace among middle-age, and even younger, populations (Gormley & Brodzinsky, 1993). A high, sustained rate of teenage pregnancies has created a pool of first-time grandparents who are healthy, working, and energetically and actively pursuing their own interests.

---

[2]This name and all others in this chapter are pseudonyms.

Each year, more than 1 million teenagers become pregnant (Forrest & Singh, 1990). Approximately 50% of these pregnancies result in a live birth—the number is reduced due to miscarriages and abortions (about 45% of pregnant teens abort their pregnancies, which accounts for approximately 30% of all abortions performed). Significantly more teen mothers have decided to remain single than in the past. In 1970, about 30% of teenage mothers were unmarried; by 1990, that figure had risen to more than 67% of all teen births (Usdansky, 1993). In 1982, births to unmarried teenagers accounted for about 7% of all births; by 1990, births to unmarried teenagers represented more than 30% of all births—a fourfold increase (Forrest & Singh, 1990). Fewer than 5% of offspring of unmarried teen mothers were released for adoption in the 1980s (McGee, 1982).

Teen mothers, as compared to older mothers, continue to depend on their own mothers for support (Garcia-Coll, Hoffman, & Oh, 1987). Furstenberg, Levine, and Brooks-Gum (1990) conducted a study in Baltimore on African-American teen mothers and found that none of these teen mothers were living alone, and most were still living with their parent(s).

This study attempts to reveal the patterns characteristic of the tenacious relationships between mother and daughter by highlighting the life stories of several representative informants. Twenty-six women between the ages of 29 and 34, living in a large metropolitan city, were surveyed regarding early grandparenting. Several women were identified through referrals from human service agencies serving low-income populations and the others were referred by other young grandmothers. All 26 women were African American. Six of the women participated in in-depth interviews in which participants were encouraged to share their day-to-day involvement in the lives of their daughters and grandchildren. All of the women had lived within a 6-mile radius of each other all of their lives. The oldest was 34 years old.

The stories that follow illustrate how these young grandmothers constructed tenacious relationships with their daughters, relationships that became vitally important to the well-being of the single-parent teenage mothers. These stories confirm research findings that suggest that the maternal grandmother, in particular, is a powerful influence in promoting a sense of well-being in teenage mothers and their children (Furstenburg & Crawford, 1978; Kivett, 1993; Matthews & Sprey, 1985). The following themes display the texture of these tenacious relationships as experienced in the lives of the young grandmothers.

ACCEPTANCE OF THE PREGNANCY

A majority of the young grandmothers, when asked how they each found out about their daughters' pregnancies, indicated that they "guessed it" or were told by someone other than their daughters. The remaining daughters told their mothers themselves. The verification of the pregnancy caused some grandmothers to initially become angry, a common parental response (Osofsky & Osofsky, 1978). Typical first comments made to the daughters following the revelation of the pregnancy were embittered comments like, *"You had everything to use and you didn't"*; or questioning remarks such as, *"Why in the world did you do something like this?"* Cleo vividly remembered the night that Alisa admitted that she was pregnant. *"I cried. I didn't want her to be pregnant. I was angry for doing this. I felt like my chances for ever going back to school were over. I still think that's why my other kids just can't let this happen."*

However, temporary feelings of hurt or general distress often changed to delight and happiness about the prospect of having a new child in the home. Once they had time to think about the situation, there was absolutely no hesitancy or variation among the opinions of the grandmothers on what they wanted their daughters to do about the pregnancy. Every one of them said, *"Keep the baby and live with me! We'll take care of it, don't worry."*

Cleo believes that God gives us these children. She said, *"As sad as I was that Alisa became pregnant, I never considered adoption or abortion."* Cleo found out about Alisa's pregnancy around the fourth month of gestation. Cleo said she guessed about the pregnancy because *"Alisa became quiet and avoided me; she didn't look me in the eye. I figured something was wrong and one night, when Alisa came through the door, I just asked if she was pregnant. The next day I made her go the clinic to see a doctor and get vitamins. I made her eat good to take care of that baby."* The other grandmothers interviewed held Cleo's opinion that, in their families, abortion really was not an option.

Cleo took responsibility for the unborn child. She saw to it that Alisa ate properly and kept her visits at the clinic. It was she who took Alisa to the hospital, who held her hand as Alisa gave birth, and who held the baby in the operating room. Jamal's father came to visit the next day. It did not take long for Cleo and each of the women in this study to realize that not only was her daughter having a baby, but also that she was becoming a grandmother.

GRANDPARENTING/FIRST TIME TO PARENT

The grandmothers indicated that the grandchildren presented them with the opportunity to parent, an experience they were denied when their mothers took over the rearing of their own children. The young grandmothers felt that the years had provided them with improved parenting skills and maturity of action. They now believed that they were more capable "mothers" than their daughters—the same message that had been conveyed to them by their mothers. The surveyed grandmothers specifically stated that they perceived their daughters to be too young or too ill-prepared to adequately care for their children. The young grandmothers acknowledged that these were the same reasons given to them when their babies were raised by their mothers.

The grandmothers were unanimous in saying that they were upset with themselves for not taking advantage of the opportunity provided them by their mothers who cared for their babies and tried hard to encourage them to stay in school. As one grandmother reflected, *"What was I thinking? Life was supposed to be fun. I didn't worry about the future. I didn't even worry about taking care of my son. All I did was hang out with boys, and then I got pregnant again."*

Alisa shares a special bond with Cleo's mother, a bond that was common with all the daughters. Cleo and Alisa lived with Cleo's mother until Alisa was 9 years old. Cleo saw her mother raise Alisa and, *"In many ways I felt more like she was my sister than my mother. As long as we lived with my mother, she did everything for Alisa. She brought her to school on her first day, carried her to church when she was a baby. . . . I was out with my friends and Alisa was with my mom. . . . After we moved out, Alisa went back to visit frequently."*

Another grandmother shared that *"I never did feel like I had mothered my own daughter. . . . I took more care of my younger son. . . . I feel more like a mom to him."*

Teary eyed, another grandmother said, *"I always resented my mom. I even got real angry with her for being so close to my daughter. I felt she wanted her all to herself. I'm just beginning to understand and appreciate all the sacrifices she made for me. I owe her a lot."*

Cleo expressed resentment that her mother spends so much time with Alisa, saying that Alisa is most likely to look to her grandmother than to her for nurturing guidance. Alisa says that her grandmother did not know about the pregnancy before Cleo, but Cleo wonders if that is true.

Somehow, all of the grandmothers were surprised when their daughters got pregnant. Knowing how difficult their own lives have been, and all the preaching they have done to their daughters, each declared that this is *"not the way it was supposed to be."*

GRANDMOTHER'S LIFE—NEW DEMANDS

In each instance, the young grandmothers put their own lives on hold, making daily sacrifices to help their daughters through the pregnancies. In each case used in this study, the daughters have remained single and have not married the fathers of the children. Throughout the pregnancy and after the birth of their child, it was the grandmothers who took charge. These young grandmothers made arrangements for their daughters to get prenatal care and in all cases were with their daughters when they gave birth. Few fathers were present during the births of their children. In two cases, the great grandmother was also present when her granddaughter gave birth. The grandmothers added that they were the ones who made the appointments for the child for check ups, shots, and so on. Cleo said, *"Since Alisa is in school when the clinic is open, I have taken him every time when he needs to go. Alisa ain't never gone with him even once."* One grandmother said, *"When my grandson was born he was a preemie and he had to stay in the hospital for 10 days. My daughter went home the second day. I stayed day and night the first 3 days 'til they were sure everything was okay. My daughter came to see him but she had to ride the bus and she wasn't feeling too good. She couldn't breastfeed him or nothing, so I just stayed. . . . I had to call where I worked and told them I couldn't come in, I almost got fired, but then I worked extra when I went back."*

The grandmothers were concerned about what would happen to their other children. Cleo said, *"Alisa's younger brother and two sisters help me care for Jamal. When my youngest isn't in school she takes my grandson for walks and plays with him. She's 6 years old, and it's like she has her own real-life baby-doll."*

Other grandmothers say that the other children have expressed resentment because of less money, the baby crying, less space, and the lack of time that the grandmother has to spend with her own children. Painfully, one grandmother shared that her younger daughter told her, *"Sometimes I hate that baby, you spend all of your time with her, she seems to be more important than I am."* The grandmothers feel like they are walking a delicate tightrope in balancing their time. *"The person who loses time is me"* stated one grandmother. *"I try to do everything I used to for my children, then I add in my grandchild. I've had to give up sleep and some of the church services. Sometimes I'm so tired, but then I know what I have to do."* Another grandmother believed prayer helped her find the energy to keep going. *"I'm a young woman, I'm 33 years old, but sometimes I feel so old and that I've already lived a lifetime. My daughter's English teacher is 35 years old and having her first child. I can't imagine not having all of those responsibilities all these years. Imagine, 35 and first child.*

GRANDMOTHERS' DREAMS

Cleo lives in a three-bedroom apartment, with a living room, dining room, and one bathroom, on the third floor of a housing project. Cleo said this is the largest apartment she has ever lived in. Cleo had pictures of her family hanging on the wall behind the sofa. She shared:

> *Someday I hope to have high school diplomas hanging up there, too. I thought about getting my GED, but that isn't possible now that WE have Jamal. Someday, don't know when, I'll get mine. . . . My kids are going to get their diplomas, they have to, they can't get no where without them. . . . Alisa, I told her she's got to stay in school, I'll help her any way I can. She's a good girl, she's my oldest, if she gets her diploma then the other kids will too.*

Cleo expressed concern that Alisa not become pregnant again. *"I feel real caught sometimes. I want to make it easy for her to stay in school. But I don't want to make it so easy that she might not worry about having another one. . . . I brought her down to the clinic and I told her she had to take those pills."* Before Alisa got pregnant, Cleo went to work in a nearby grocery store. She had hoped to save money and one day get a home funded by the government. She felt that she had to quit her job to take care of the baby. Just recently, Cleo spoke with another young grandmother who offered to work out an arrangement so that they could babysit for each others' grandchildren and each could get a part-time job. Cleo expressed her strong belief that she had to be there for her daughter. By watching Jamal, Alisa was free to continue her education.

Cleo talked about her hopes for her children, her grandchildren, and herself:

I've always been single, but I would like to get married sometime and move out of here—but I got four kids. Sometimes I dream that I'll move, but I know that I will probably stay here forever. I want it to be different for my kids. I want to get them out of here. I love my daughter and my grandson. When I hold Jamal, I tell him how he's gon' to be a doctor. I even tell him that I'll help pay for him to go to medical school—think of that, a doctor in the family. I want it to happen real bad. I've gotta help Alisa so she can be an English teacher. I want to get my GED before Alisa graduates from college.

GRANDMOTHER-DAUGHTER RELATIONSHIP

Cleo, like so many young grandmothers, wants to be there to support and encourage her children. Yet, with this, is the delicate balance of realizing the responsibility of the daughter to her child. Although all of the grandmothers declared that their daughters were appreciative of the caring their mothers were showing toward their children, the daughters' own roles became unclear. Several grandmothers acknowledged that there was conflict over whose child this really was. One grandmother stated, *"My daughter complains that I make all the decisions, but she is never around to make them. She goes to school, and she goes to her friends' houses and has a little part-time job. When she is home she wants to be in charge of her kid, but it doesn't work that way with me. I'm doing 95% of all the work, so I told her I make 95% of all the decisions."* Another grandmother said

She plays with her daughter like she's a cute little doll or even a puppy—then she wants to walk away and do her thing. I tell her that her thing is now changing diapers, doing laundry, stuff like that. She likes the fun part

of her daughter, but I tell her there is a lot more to raising a kid than fixin' her hair and walking around the neighborhood and showin' her off. She even told me what to do in the beginning, but I made sure that stopped real quick, if you know what I mean.

Cleo said Alisa did help with Jamal, but what frustrated her the most was all the running around she wanted to do. *"I love Jamal and I love my daughter and I'd do anything to help her. But when she's runnin' around with her friends and not doing her homework—well that makes me mad, real mad. Education, that's so important. I wish that girl would just understand how important it is."* Later in the conversation Cleo reiterated her concern about Alisa, *"Alisa and I argue sometimes—not so bad though. Mostly we fuss about her not stayin' home and not doin' her homework. I want her to get real good grades; they haven't been so good lately 'cause she goes around with her friends too much."*

FATHER'S ROLE

According to Cleo, Jamal's father rarely comes to the house to spend time with him. *"He doesn't play with him or show any interest in Jamal. He hasn't paid for anything. My grandson needs a dad. I pray that someday Alisa will get her education, get married, and get out of this neighborhood."* This was typical of the role of the fathers of their daughters' children—in and out of the picture. *"I know I shouldn't say this, but I wish he wouldn't come around at all. I'm scared to death he'll get her pregnant again. . . . I know she really cares for him, but I don't know if I can handle another baby."* This grandmother also shared, *"He doesn't have a job and he's been in trouble with the police. He's no good for my daughter."*

Another grandmother expressed anger toward her granddaughter's father. *"He comes struttin' in here with a teddy bear or something, plays with her for a little while, takes her outside in the cold and then I stay up with her all night long while she's coughing. Where's he . . . I'll leave that to your imagination."*

Cleo told Alisa, *"A good man may marry you with one child, but he doesn't want two or three kids from another man, he wants his own children with you. . . . There is a girl who lived down the street and she married a guy who is a policeman. She had one child, and they moved into a nice house. . . . I keep reminding Alisa of her."* Of the 26 women interviewed, none of the women wanted their daughters to marry the father of their daughters' children.

EXTENDED FAMILY SUPPORT

The extended family also shares a significant role in these young grandparenting situations. Cleo's own mother lives merely three blocks from her, and two of Cleo's three sisters live nearby as well. They are willing to babysit Jamal to help Alisa stay in school. Cleo's own mother babysits for her great grandson, but she is already rearing a child of Cleo's younger sister. All of the young grandmothers had immediate family that lived nearby and helped out when needed. Cleo described an intricate bartering system that she as well as other family members utilize.

> *If I have a chair, I give it to her (my sister), and I know about how much it's worth, and then when I need some clothes or my kids need something, she might buy it for us. I may give her three things before she gives back one. When Jamal was born we didn't have to nearly buy nothing 'cause so many people owed me. My one niece gave me a crib, somebody else who owed me gave me a stroller, and that's how it goes. The favors went to Jamal instead of me. That's okay. We wouldn't make it if we all didn't help each other. There really isn't much exchange of money, but we're all here to help each other out.*

Another young grandmother put it this way, *"About all we got here is our family. . . . We know that we have to help each other. . . . You don't ask questions, ya just try to help each other any way you can. If somebody in the family gets a little extra money, we share it with our family."*

Due to the proximity of family living in the same area, family members are readily available to babysit for each other. Cleo said that because she already is home with Jamal so much, she babysits for other children in the family.

SELF-SUFFICIENCY

Of the 26 grandmothers, 3 were able to maintain close to full-time jobs, and one of the daughters worked. All the families utilized free clinics, welfare, and church support. Still, they were always falling short. The increased financial burden of the new child meant less for the other children in the family. Finances were a constant source of worry and concern for the grandmothers. Only one family received any support from the child's father, and that was from his mother and it was sporadic. It was the grandmother who ended up sacrificing small personal treats for things such as diapers and school supplies for the other children.

> *Before Jamal was born, once a year I took my children to the zoo and we'd have a picnic, and then the big thing was the church-sponsored trip to an*

amusement park. I'd save up all year, but we had such a good time. We can't go anymore. We haven't gone the past two years.

Another grandmother described how much she enjoyed singing in her church choir and traveling to other cities to sing in churches. *"I can't afford to go anymore. The church deacons said that they could pay for me, but that's not right. . . . It's just a sacrifice I have to make right now."*

Each grandmother recounted small ways that she is able to bring in extra funds. One grandmother cleans the halls in her apartment building, another has found a job working the night shift part time. One grandmother works for a community agency each week sorting clothes. She gets any clothes she wants free.

The grandmothers were proud that they were finding ways to make money. All of them were also using some public funding. As one grandmother said, *"I don't like it, but it has to be. . . . This comes back to education. When my kids get their diplomas, they'll be able to get jobs and we'll all get off of welfare. . . . I don't know anybody in their right mind who'd want to live here and be on welfare. Everybody wants to get a job and get out of here."*

Although individuals surveyed mentioned churches, medical facilities, and selected social services as being somewhat helpful, nearly half of the grandmothers indicated that the families had to be self-sufficient. Problems most frequently mentioned by the grandmothers were difficulties dealing with social service/welfare agencies (e.g., problems with transfer of payments and extension of benefits for the grandchild and negative attitudes of caseworkers), obstacles in the continued education of the daughter (e.g., lack of affordable and convenient day care, scheduling, inappropriate counseling), and pressures resulting from financial shortages.

The educational system remained steadfastly neutral, similar to the schools mentioned by Heydt (chapter 5), both during and after the pregnancy. Administrators and teachers did not drive the students out of the programs, but neither did they do anything to help the teenagers stay in school. One grandmother shared that her daughter was given no assignments by the teachers the last couple of weeks before the baby was born. *"She missed nearly 4 weeks. There ain't no way that girl could catch up when she got back. I called the principal and she said she tried to get the work but she never did. She dropped out of school. She just couldn't get back into it."*

Cleo knew of several instances where individual teachers acknowledged the inflexibility of the structure of schooling and actually suggested the girls drop out of school. *"No one ever called here when Alisa gave birth. I don't know why they wouldn't want her there, she's smart and all. Alisa's friend helped her to keep up."* Except for Cleo, no one else tenaciously held Alisa's attention on schooling. Cleo insisted she find a way to stay in school.

The steadfast neutrality of the educational institutions facilitates a structure of predictability and uniformity, thus excluding the messiness of life's crises. In the opinion of the young grandmothers in this study, the schools' efforts fell considerably short in meeting the needs of these women, their daughters, and their grandchildren. Cleo said that most of her support has come through her church. Only one person at school, an English teacher, ever calls about things—good or bad.

SUPPORT FOR EDUCATIONAL GOALS

Nevertheless, education seemed to be at the center of all the grandmothers' seeming willingness to sacrifice their own lives for that of their daughters. Of the women interviewed, only one had a high school diploma. She had become pregnant her junior year and her mother took care of her son so that she could finish high school. The remaining grandmothers all quit school while in high school, after having their own children. They all continued for varying lengths of time, but none were able to complete their diplomas. They stated how much they now regret it.

> *There was no real excuse, I wasn't interested, I felt like I had already ruined my life, so why bother? My mama was taking care of my daughter, so I can't say that was an excuse. I didn't see that a high school diploma was that big of a deal back then. . . . I sure do now!*

Cleo shared her consistent willingness to readily make sacrifices for Alisa to stay in school,

> *My mama had a ninth-grade education. I was in the 11th grade when I quit going to school. Alisa is going to get her high school diploma, and so will my other kids. I'm goin' to make 'em stay in school. When Jamal got sick early in the year, she wanted to stay at home and take care of him. I wouldn't let her. She belongs in school. . . . She just can't quit.*

The grandmothers all still wanted their GEDs. Cleo said, *"Even if I have to take Jamal with me to the classes, I'm going to get my GED. I know I'm smart and I could get better jobs if I had it. I know I will have it one day."*

Many of the grandmothers shared their desires for their daughters to continue on to college. Cleo had told Alisa, who was then a junior in high school, that she could continue to live at home until she graduates. *"If my girl goes to college, then I'll care for Jamal. She can even live at college, maybe. I want her to stay in school. She's a smart girl. One of her teachers said that she could probably help Alisa get into college. I'll do anything to help her."*

Cleo described getting on a bus with Alisa and her brother and taking them to a nearby college:

> *He just walked around and looked at the buildin's. I showed them Black kids walking around. Alisa was about 7 and her brother 5. I told them they*

were smart and one day other moms would be pointing to them when they were on the college campus and telling their kids to be just like my Alisa and Tobias. . . . I pray every day that my kids can go to college.

Grandmother after grandmother told about getting good grades in school and how their own pregnancies curtailed their dreams.

I was the smartest kid in math in my class—teachers were always braggin' on me. I would dream about gettin' a college diploma and bein' a girl engineer . . . making lots of money. I could see myself walkin' into a real pretty house with a lawn and a front porch with a swing, pickin' up my mama and sayin', 'Look where I live.' All that ended when I got pregnant, . . . but it isn't going to end for my daughter. She's got my math brain. . . . That girl's going stay in school. She says she wants to get a scholarship for college and be a nurse. . . . I do anything to make her dreams come true.

"*I keep telling my younger kids to see what is happening to my oldest and not to let it happen to them.*" Cleo indicated that her younger children get "preached to a lot." "*I told them that I can't take care of all your children. Sometimes I laugh and tell them, 'You is suppose to take care of me when I'm an old woman, its not me suppose to be taken' care of your kids.*"

CONCLUSION

The roles of the young grandmothers dramatically differ from that of the traditional grandparent in that they have become the primary caretakers of their grandchildren rather than serving as an occasional, supplemental custodian. The usual pattern for this group is that the young grandmothers have assumed near total responsibility for rearing their grandchildren immediately following birth. This arrangement takes on the characteristics of an informal adoption process, with the birth mother living in the same household as her child but abdicating many of her expected functions, until the daughter reaches 18 years of age and/or establishes her own residence supported by a spouse, work, or social support funds. In many instances, the young grandmother continues as *significant other* in the life of the child, even after the daughter and grandchild have left her home and immediate caretaking, supplying financial, moral, and emotional support throughout early childhood development.

With primary responsibility for grandchildren under the age of 3, the grandmothers could only see years of self-denial for themselves. Self-denial was coupled with tenacious insistence on education for their daughters that may result in the daughters remaining in school and vicariously fulfilling their own dreams for an education and a different future. Cleo and the other young grandmothers believed that through their sacrifices, the lives of their children and grandchildren *had* to be better.

4

Survival Patterns Among Unemancipated Independent Living Teenagers

Joel Milgram
University of Cincinnati
Nancy Briton
Harvard University

This chapter examines the lives of high school students who live on their own without adult or agency supervision. This study, based on interviews with more than 30 high school students and older adolescents, illustrates how tenacity can and sometimes must be generated within one's peer group or within oneself. These youngsters, pushouts from mostly affluent families, actually appear to construct a tenacious relationship with themselves. They are determined not to be dropouts. Economics makes the final call as to whether they will succeed. Note, again, the paradoxical nature of tenacity. The school officials know that these underage students have not been declared "emancipated minors," and that they are not living at home. They should report them to children's services. But, the institution of schooling is tenaciously neutral, involving itself in the internal affairs of school, and not the outside affairs of people's daily lives.
—Editors

* * *

Brian and his dad argued all the time, mostly about drugs and music. Eventually Brian was "kind of ejected" and lived with friends. An attempted reconciliation failed and Brian decided he could make it on his own.

Most high school students in America leave their parents' home in the morning and return sometime after school. But there are others who leave and return to their own apartments, where there exists no adult or agency supervision. Although clearly, high school students who live without any adult supervision have taken on enormous responsibilities not usually required of people their age, in a number of cases the students themselves perceive their status as an improvement over living with their parents. More common, however, is a story of a difficult personal adjustment and a sense of abandonment, even when the split with the family was student-initiated, as the adolescents attempt to adjust to an independent living situation. Most of the students of high school age who venture out on their own will drop out of school. But some do not. The students described here were determined to complete their high school education, with or without parental support and with or without the support and/or knowledge of their schools. Their tenacity emerges as their stories are detailed.

THE STUDY

This investigation examined the survival patterns of adolescents who live on their own without adult or agency supervision and remain full-time high school students. Although there is substantial literature on dropouts, pushouts, adolescent homeless, and runaways, there appears to be no published research on this small group of students who, despite the hardships caused by separation from their families, remain in school until graduation. The research originated from our theoretical interests in adolescent development, risk and resilience, and family systems.

The overall objectives of the project were to learn (a) why these students did not drop out of school despite the high-risk situation they found themselves in; (b) what the circumstances were that led up to their independent living status; (c) what their living conditions were like; and, (d) the extent to which their high schools were aware of their circumstances.

Twenty-two adolescents, nine high school personnel from six schools, and five parents from four families participated in this study. The adolescents were in two categories: those who were currently enrolled in high school and had been living independently for at least one school year (9 participants), and those who had graduated from high school within the previous 12 months and who lived independently for at least 1 year while attending high school full time (15 participants). Seven of the adolescents were female and 15 were male. Recruitment took place via notices on telephones near high schools, direct contact in the field, and notices on college campuses and in fast food restaurants.

Interviews with current high school students took place in public locations such as libraries, restaurants, and street corners. High school graduates were interviewed at work locations or university offices. Initial interviews were 1 hour in duration, during which time a questionnaire was completed and an interview was recorded using a semistructured interview protocol. For some of the participants, second interviews took place in home settings. All adolescent participants were paid per interview session. The interviews were conducted in Cincinnati, Ohio or Boston, Massachusetts.

The stories of Brian, Kelley, Cindy, and Dwight[1] reveal the circumstances that caused them to live independently and, despite being on their own, to refuse to drop out of high school. At an age where society still considers these participants to be children, that is, unemancipated minors, these four stories illustrate the tenacity of self-caring. We chose these particular stories because each one represents one of the following four kinds of adolescents we found to be living on their own while maintaining full-time status in high school:

1. Adolescents who were asked to leave the family home (Dwight).
2. Adolescents who were abandoned (Kelley).
3. Adolescents who initiated their departure (Brian).
4. Adolescents who left by mutual consent (Cindy).

DWIGHT'S STORY

Among our participants who fell into the category of "Being asked to leave the family home," none experienced the event as abruptly as Dwight.

Dwight was 16, a sophomore in high school in Boston, and homosexual. *"Not a great place to be gay,"* he laughed during one of our interviews. Dwight decided to tell his parents rather than continue to keep his homosexuality a secret. *"A friend of mine kind of pushed me into telling (my parents) perhaps earlier than I felt comfortable with."*

Dwight reported that his relationship with his parents at this time was *"not particularly close."* His older brother had had an automobile accident the year before and was institutionalized.

> They kind of had to pull away from the rest of the family and concentrate on him. It wasn't as much of an issue for my sisters because they are older than I am. I'm the youngest in the family. It kind of left me in a weird position. When I was younger, I was a little spoiled, and because I was the baby and all of a sudden, at the age of 14, I had to fend for myself, not getting very much attention at all because of the accident, when [my brother] got hurt. . . I felt cheated out of something, but I really didn't know what it was.
>
> "I told them [about my homosexuality], individually. First my mom, then my dad. I expected my father to be very belligerent about it, and very

---

[1]Names used are pseudonyms.

angry, and I expected my mother to be very supportive. It kind of turned out the other way around. . . . I was very up front with my mother, and she went off to her room crying, and got very upset. I went to the living room and told my father, and expected a strong backlash. He just sat down and said "okay." . . . As I was talking to my father, my mother came down the stairs and basically said, "I can't handle this. You can't stay here."

I kind of panicked, and I didn't know what to do, so I called a friend of mine who said, "why don't you stay with me tonight, and let them cool off?" And when I came back the next day, my mother had packed my suitcases. They were just sitting there.

Dwight spent the next night with his sympathetic older sisters in their apartment, and then spent several additional days with friends. By the second week, he had found an apartment with two friends who were both a year older. Dwight found a part-time job at a pizzeria and was able to pay for rent and food. For the next 2 years, he attended high school, worked, and survived. The worst part of living on his own was

> *not being able to afford things that I felt were necessities. There would be weeks when I had to decide whether I was going to buy food or pay my portion of the electric bill. You know, I really wanted that food, but the roommates I had at the time were really firm about paying bills on time. I mooched when I could, but the money part was really tough. I got to the point where I hated having to work to survive. I hated the situation I was in, and it took me awhile to learn that the only one who can do it is me, and the person who can help me out is me.*

Dwight had little communication with either parent from that time on. *"For the first 9 months of living on my own, my parents cut off all contact. For the first couple of days, I tried to talk to them, and tried to come over to the house, but my mother had the locks changed."* The only area of agreement was that the high school he attended should not know about his independent living situation. Dwight figured his parents were embarrassed and did not want anyone to know that he didn't live at home and why.

> *The first few months were really trying because I honestly thought that someone was going to find out and there was going to be a big problem. I was afraid. I wouldn't take any time off from school. Actually, my senior year I had perfect attendance. Even if I was sick I went in. I was afraid that if I was out they would call my parents' house to verify I was home, so I never missed a day.*

Dwight did not confide in anyone at his school. He feared that the school would have to report the situation, and he would end up in *"some kind of home for delinquent youth."* He signed his parents' names when he needed to, continued to attend school, and graduated on time. His parents did not come to his graduation; a grandmother did. *"That was kind of a victory on my part because somehow, somewhere along the line, someone told my grandmother and she showed up. That made me very happy. She told me she was very proud of me because I had done it myself. "*

Did Dwight ever consider dropping out of school?

Oh, yes, I had to pick up more hours of work, about 35 hours a week, and weekends, so . . . my studies suffered. I had always been an A or A- student, and [my grades] went down. There was a few times when I thought it would be easy to give it all up, but I had a good friend, and I would talk to him about it more than anyone else. He had dropped out in his junior year and he was the one who basically said, "look, just finish. . . . You only have a couple months. Just finish. " He said it was really important and that I would find out how important later on.

Dwight says he is still paying back some debts he incurred during that time. *"People have been very patient. A good friend of mine lent me $400, and it took me almost a year and a half to pay him back. It strained a lot of friendships."*

Dwight is currently a part-time student at a college in the Boston area. *"When I turned 18, a friend told me I could apply for financial aid for college without my parents. I did, and I am now majoring in accounting. I would like you to know,"* he told us during our last interview with him, *"I like the person that I have become. I'm a lot stronger than I was, and understand what it means to be self-reliant. I know what has to get done and what you have to go through to get it done."* Dwight rarely sees his parents anymore. He sees himself finishing school someday and earning a decent living. We asked Dwight, as we asked all of the participants, if he knew any high school students who live on their own. *"Sure,"* he replied, *"lots."*

Dwight did not choose to live on his own. His parents made that choice for him. Dwight possessed some qualities, however, that we believe contributed to his resiliency. First, he was a good student before his expulsion from his parents' home. Although he admitted that his grades dropped due to the added responsibilities of independent living, he could maintain acceptable grades while on his own. Second, he had a source of income. His job, although low paying, afforded him at least a subsistence wage. Third, he had someone to talk to and encourage him to complete high school. He spoke of a friend who reminded him that he could in fact reach this goal. We found these themes of previous academic achievement, economic means, and social support to be consistent predictors of success throughout our interviews.

KELLEY'S STORY

If many adolescents have unfulfilled needs, we can assume that their parents also have them. Kelley's mother fulfilled her need to be on her own by simply "taking off."

Kelley's story is different from Dwight's because Kelley did not leave home, her mother left Kelley. She and her mother moved to Florida from Michigan after her parents' divorce. At the end of her freshman year in high school, Kelley's mother announced she was ready to fulfill a lifelong dream. In the driveway of their home was a large, brand new Winnebago, and her mother proudly announced: "I am ready to do my Winnebago thing . . . to tour the United States for as long as I have a mind to. " Kelley announced that she was not too excited about leaving because they just had arrived a year ago and she was beginning to make a lot of new friends. *"No one wants to leave in the middle of their high school years,"* Kelley told us, *"so when my mother said that I could stay and live on my own I said GREAT. I was 16 for God's sake . . . what did I know?"*

Kelley's mom sold the house and bought a smaller townhouse for Kelley to live in. Although a college student was initially hired to live with Kelley, that arrangement fell apart within 3 months. Kelley's mother stayed in touch with her by phone once a week and sent money regularly. At Christmas time, Kelley would fly to visit with her mother. *"I would go wherever she was with her Winnebago—California, Colorado, Canada."* This arrangement continued for the rest of Kelley's high school years. So at the beginning of her sophomore year, Kelley was on her own. She told us that for the first year she had frequent parties and *"lots of kids stayed over, . . . and a boyfriend stayed for a good six months."* But by the time Kelley entered her junior year *"the novelty wore off . . . I had to start locking the doors so not everybody could come in the house. . . ."* Kelley regained control of her living space, and, for the last half of her junior year and all of her senior year, she was the only one who lived in her home.

Besides her every other week phone conversations with her mother, Kelley remained in contact with her father who lived in the midwest. They talked on the phone *"a couple times a year"*; her father was *"very upset"* when he first learned that Kelley's mother left and she was on her own. He did not offer to move down to be with his daughter nor did Kelley ever consider living with her father. She and her father *"totally don't agree on anything . . . like I'm a female and I belong in the kitchen. . . ."*

It was about this time that Kelley started to re-evaluate her relationship with her mother. Kelley told us, *"I realized my mom really didn't care about me much, and that started to bother me a lot. Everything she did was for herself."*

Kelley reported that her high school counselors were aware of her situation, but it did not seem to present any particular problems. It was well known that Kelley's parents would not be available for any conferences and Kelley believed there never was a need for one anyway. Kelley thinks that the reason her high school teachers and counselors did not make a fuss over her situation was because *"I remained well dressed and well fed and didn't cause any trouble . . . and I was never poor, money was not a problem."* During her junior year, her grades remained at the B or C level *"just as they were when my mom was home, but in my senior year, I discovered that if I studied, I got As."* So she studied. *"My senior year I got straight As."*

When we first met Kelley, she had just started her freshman year at college having graduated high school 4 months previously. She was required to live in a freshman dorm her first year and we asked her how she felt about that. *"Well, I'm a lot more mature than most of the other kids . . . most of them are away from home for the first time and going nuts. I did that already."* She has limited phone contact with her mother and made all the arrangements herself regarding college. Kelley says she is angrier now about being left to finish high school on her own than she was as a high school student. *"When you are 16 you are supposed to be with someone, aren't you? . . . When I was younger I didn't know it was unusual. Now I know."*

BRIAN'S STORY

For many of our participants, it was not clear whether they left the family home voluntarily or were asked to leave. When family conflicts reach a critical level, it becomes a blur and no one can recall who walked away from whom.

Brian moved with his family to a New England resort town when he was starting his junior year. His older siblings had already moved away to attend college. At the end of the school year, Brian said, he was *"kind of ejected from the house because I wasn't getting along with my dad, but it was really mutual."* He lived with a friend and that friend's family for the summer. At the end of the summer, he and his father agreed that *"it would be in my best interest"* to return home and finish his senior year.

Brian agreed to see a psychologist with his parents to work on his relationship with his father because *"you know, I figured that would be fair."* But Brian's experience with the psychologist was *"a terrible day. . . . It started with the three of us in the room . . . then he asked my parents to leave, and then he got into my history, my friends, my experimentation (with drugs). . . . Before I answered [his questions], I asked, 'Is this between you and me; or you, me, and my parents?' and he said it was strictly confidential."* Brian said, "At first, it was good to talk about it all, but then he called my parents back in the room, and he didn't come right out and say things that I told him, but he inferred them, and referred to them." Brian feels that the psychologist *"betrayed my trust"* and *"just sided with my parents. . . . He didn't know where I was coming from."* After that one session, Brian said, *"They wanted me to come back, but I adamantly refused."*

Instead, Brian and his friend, who was in a similar situation, got an apartment "*so I could finish high school there.*" Brian's family did not provide any financial support, so Brian got various jobs. "*For a while, I was working three jobs. . . . I was a bellman [at a hotel], and then I would go from there and . . . work in a bagel shop . . . or at the town hall putting stuff into their computer.*" Brian earned enough from his part-time jobs to pay for rent and food.

Brian felt that living on his own had its advantages. "*I could get things done. . . . Whenever I was home with my parents, all I ever did was want to leave . . . I would leave and go hang out and be . . . unproductive, whereas in my apartment, I was comfortable, and I had no problem staying home. I stopped going out a lot and I started . . . getting stuff done. It was a much more relaxed atmosphere.*

But the food was definitely lacking. . . . It was basically peanut butter and jelly three times a day. I did work at a bagel shop so that helped out a lot."

He didn't think the school was aware that he was living on his own. He remembered one time "*I had tardiness or something and I couldn't get a note from my folks.*" Instead, he simply served detention for an unexcused tardiness. Otherwise, Brian reported no administrative problems. He used his father's address on all school forms.

Brian's mother was, he said, "*kind of the mediator between me and my dad.*" It "*upset her*" that he was not living at home, "*and my dad thought it was a bad idea that I wasn't there too, but . . . we just didn't get along.*" Brian's problems with his father revolved around Brian's "*friends and lifestyle,*" he reported, meaning drugs. Brian admits to having used drugs, but his father "*assumed it was a lot worse than it was.*"

Surprisingly, Brian said that his relationship with his father is "*pretty good*" now. "*They realized that I was on my own and could do it.*" In fact, Brian spent the last summer living at home with his parents "*and it was great.*"

Brian is 19 now and in college, majoring in music. His parents help out with tuition. Brian thinks he will change majors from music performance to technical engineering. His father is an engineer, and, according to Brian, "*a very wise man . . . ignorant to my feelings, but I didn't realize what a smart guy he was.*"

CINDY'S STORY

When divorced parents compete for their adolescents' favor, new options for the youngster become available. Live with one, or the other, or strike the best deal possible?

Cindy was 17 when she was interviewed for our study. Her parents were divorced when she was in the sixth grade, and Cindy went to live with her mother.

When my mom got remarried [when Cindy was in the 10th grade], she got really distracted and was not really into her kids at that time, I guess, so I moved in with my dad for a year of high school. Then he moved to California [from New England], and it was either I can move in with my dad or my mom, or move out on my own. I spoke to my dad about that, and since I had the same boyfriend for 4 years, . . . he said I could live on my own . . . with my boyfriend . . . if I moved out to California. . . . When my boyfriend and I got there, he had an apartment waiting for us."

Cindy's father *"picked out the apartment and put down the down payment, you know, the security deposit and the first month's rent, and then right after that both of us got jobs and we paid for everything ourselves."* Cindy started high school in California. She used her father's address for the school records and reported no problems with school officials. Both Cindy and her boyfriend earned enough from their jobs to remain financially independent from Cindy's father, although Cindy refers to this time of her life as *"my poor time."*

In fact, other than economic obstacles, Cindy reported few problems at all. Overall, she considered her life to be improved. Her eating habits, especially, were better than when she lived with her parents. *"When I moved out of my house, my boyfriend and I made a conscious decision to eat really well, and we did. We ate a lot of vegetables, chicken, and tofu, and rarely red meat."*

After graduation, Cindy returned to her mother's home state *"for a vacation, with the intention of going back, but I came here and had a really good time, and got along with my mom."* Cindy made a decision to not return to California or her boyfriend. Her mother works at a college where part of her benefits are tuition credits for employee dependents. Cindy decided to enroll in the college and is now a freshman, living with her mother to save money. *"It's been so long, it's kind of nice to get to know her again, even though we fight, and I do much better on my own. We argue about food shopping all the time."* She hopes to find another apartment, but does not have a job. Cindy enjoys not having to worry about *"buying food and toilet paper every day."*

Did Cindy ever consider dropping out of high school? *"Oh, no! Because both of my parents were educated, no way, even though it was stressful, I always knew I would go to college. I always knew that education is the most important thing."*

SUMMARY

Four very different stories: Dwight was thrown out of his house because of his homosexuality, Kelley's mother left her behind, Brian fought so much with his dad he felt he had to leave, and Cindy's dad encouraged her to live next to him in California. All four of these students were determined to complete their high school education, with or without the support and/or knowledge of their schools, and all four did graduate. Their tenaciousness in protecting themselves from becoming another dropout statistic shows up in different ways for each.

For all the participants, the realization that their survival is mostly up to themselves is clear. In the stories presented here, Dwight felt *"cheated out of something"* as a member of his family and felt that his hospitalized brother was the one who received all the caring. Although he found living on his own very difficult, he ultimately found that his key to survival was his realization *"that the only one who can do it is me, and the person who can help me out is me."* Kelley loved her early freedoms but learned to take control of her space when *"the novelty wore off"*: She had to start locking the doors to keep visitors out. She also learned on her own that *"if I studied, I got As."* Brian's parents, especially his father, felt he should return home, but Brian concluded it would not work and stayed away until graduation. Even though he was working three jobs to support himself, Brian felt his friends and lifestyle were just too different and he needed to be on his own. Cindy lived with her mom, her dad, and then on her own (without the anger and trauma that is part of the story of most of our participants, she appeared to choose the most practical arrangement at the time).

For some, friends played an important role in helping the participants get through difficult periods. For Dwight, it was his friends who took him in when his parents sent him away and he had no place to go, a friend who lent him $400 to buy food and pay rent, and a high school dropout friend who urged him to stick with school until graduation.

For some of our participants, aspects of their lives "improved" by living on their own. Brian reported that he could study more because he was more relaxed in his own apartment, and Cindy and her boyfriend were able to eat *"a more healthful diet."* But when we examine the stories of all of our participants, we find that most of them suffered profound economic hardships and were often discouraged. Except when parents subsidized their living (4 of 22), most of the adolescents lived in relative poverty, although easily finding part-time jobs to pay rent and buy food. Apartments were usually substandard and often did not even meet housing codes. But because the renters were unemancipated minors who preferred not to answer too many questions about where their parents were, landlords rented them spaces that city housing authorities would not approve without substantial, costly improvements. Clothing was rarely replaced, and there was very little entertainment money available. Summers meant full-time jobs and lower heating bills, but winters proved particularly difficult. All participants reported severe bouts of depression ranging from some of the time to often, and most felt they were abandoned by their parents even if the adolescent initiated the parting.

Early months for those who initiated the parting were more often than not reported as exciting; no rules, freedom to stay out late, and especially choosing one's own friends. But recapturing control of their own lives was often difficult after the initial feeling of independence. One participant learned the hard way how uncontrollable friends could become when his landlord asked him to move because of his constant partying. For most, the most pressing problem was finances, and the thing most missed was *home-cooked meals.* The most valued aspect for all was the general sense of freedom. Of the 22 participants, 17 reported that their grades either went up or basically remained unchanged. Ten stated that they studied more while living on their own because there was less tension *"in this here place . . . my place."*

Those who were interviewed while still in high school often sounded desperate and depressed during the interviews, whereas those who were interviewed after they graduated talked more philosophically about their experience. Parents who asked their children to leave reported that it was a positive situation for the adolescent, whereas parents whose children initiated the leave reported that their children suffered needlessly.

We view the four students just described as "success" stories because they finished high school under difficult conditions and they demonstrated a high degree of tenacity. They were also white, and from middle-class families. We conclude with a fifth story, the story of Kenny, also very determined to finish high school.

KENNY'S STORY

We were introduced to Kenny by a high school guidance counselor who knew of our interest in kids who lived independently. *"You can't get any more independent than this one,"* he said.

Kenny was 17 when we met him. Tall and muscular, he was a generally somber looking African-American youth. We were warned that we would not get much information about his past, although he might be willing to talk to us about his day-to-day life.

Kenny was a junior, attending a large metropolitan high school. He enrolled at the beginning of the term as a transfer student from St. Louis. He was living two blocks away from the school in a studio walk-up, and paid $105 a month rent. His family was still in St. Louis, and, as for the reasons he left to come to Cincinnati, he would only say, *"It was real important that I leave."*

As far as the school administration knew, he lived with his parents. Forms that went home for parental signature came back signed—supposedly by a parent. Kenny had confided his independent living status to his counselor, but not to any other school official.

Kenny's counselor told us that he had no intention of informing his principal about Kenny's living arrangements. Kenny had little money and held several part-time jobs to make ends meet. Besides washing dishes at a late-night diner, he stacked wooden pallets for a shipping company on Sundays. Every 3 weeks he sold his blood at a blood bank, and when he ran low on funds and it was still days away from payday, he scavenged near the trash bins of several fast food restaurants.

The only thing that Kenny would tell us about his family was that none of his older brothers or sisters nor his parents ever finished high school. Although he hinted that he would not be able to finish if he stayed home, he would not elaborate. His determination to finish school was related to his desire to become his own boss some day, rather than be someone's employee. He expressed an interest in owning a plumbing shop, and he claimed to already be a talented plumber.

We asked Kenny what he did in his spare time, and he stated that he really did not have much spare time. The apartment where he was living was slated to be torn down and he had 3 weeks to find another affordable place to live. This was his major preoccupation at the moment, although he was also concerned about a rapidly approaching social studies test. Kenny described himself as a fair student who must study very hard to get barely passing grades.

Despite the fact that he had lived in the city for about 7 months, Kenny said he had few friends. *"It would be different if I had some spare change to play with, but I need my pennies or I get hungry."* He received free medical attention at a nearby clinic but 2 months previously he was so ill for several days that he could not go to school or to any of his jobs. The blood bank even rejected him because of his high fever. Kenny said those few days' loss of salary really hit him hard and he was desperately afraid of ever missing work again.

Kenny was amused at our interest in "independents" and suggested it was really not a novel situation. He was not sure, but he believed there were lots of kids like himself who lived alone, although he admitted not all of them were in school. *"I bet the guidance counselor knows a bunch of them."*

Kenny's counselor found out about Kenny's independent status after Kenny got into a fight in the hallway and he was told that his parent was supposed to come to school to speak to the counselor. *"Had to finally tell him, and he covered for me. He's okay."*

Kenny believed he had been fortunate in that he was *"making it."* He had passing grades, a school official he could trust, and faith in the possibility that in another year and a half he would graduate from high school. We asked him if he would consider living in a county-sponsored group home as an alternative to his present living arrangement. *"Why bother?"* was his reply; *"You do that if you can't make it on your own, and that doesn't apply to me."*

Several months after our first meeting with Kenny, we returned for a follow-up visit. Kenny dropped out of school. No one knew where he was. His high school counselor, who went to Kenny's new apartment only to find it deserted, said he simply disappeared. As far as we know, Kenny was or was not one of the success stories.

SCHOOLS

The role of the high school in lending support to these independent living unemancipated minors was limited due, for the most part, to the unwillingness of the adolescents to notify their high schools that they were living on their own. Most participants feared social service interference if their living status was acknowledged. Their parents shared the same concern and often cooperated with their children in maintaining the parents' address for all official school correspondence. The majority of our participants did confide in one particular teacher or counselor about their living status and such confidences appeared to have been kept. Many of the school personnel who were confided in indicated to us that they kept an unofficial "watchful eye" on the student. Three of the participants reported being visited (with permission) by their "confidant-teachers" who were concerned about them. In one case, a participant reported receiving "bags of food on several occasions and once a little cash. . ." from a concerned counselor. In two instances, two "confidants" (a school nurse and an English teacher) stated to us that they thought the adolescents under discussion were doing a better job of caring for themselves than how they were cared for when they lived with their parents. No special support services were found to exist for independent living adolescents in any of the six schools that were associated with our study. No principal officially acknowledged the existence of unemancipated minors who were living on their own and attending school full-time, though all unofficially were aware of such students in their own school.

Both the identification of this population, as well as its study, is of educational importance. The number of young people who live on their own while attending high school is unknown. This category is not covered by the U.S. census. Furthermore, adolescent development, when viewed as a series of psychosocial stages reflected in an individual's reaction to psychosocial crises, gets put to the test with the premature separation from the family. The ability to survive on one's own at an early age suggests that for some, traditional stage theory can be hurried along out of necessity.

The interaction between the independent adolescent and the high school raises a number of ethical and legal issues. Under what conditions should high school officials intervene in the lives of unemancipated minors? If the minor appears to be doing a better job of self-rearing than the parent, should noninterference be the rule? What kind of counseling should a school district provide such a student? What additional support systems should be made available to them? If a student confides to a particular teacher, is the teacher under any legal obligation to make a report? These questions have yet to be addressed by most school districts.

The first four stories retold in this chapter were success stories. That is, Dwight, Brian, Cindy, and Kelley all graduated from high school. Their tenacity in caring for themselves contributed greatly to their success. But we interviewed adolescents who were still in high school, and we did not know at the time if they would graduate. We could guess that many, like Kenny, would not. There are too many obstacles barring most young people from making it on their own. Clearly, support systems are needed at the local and state levels to ensure that the caring for adolescents in unusual circumstances is not left only to the adolescents themselves.

ACKNOWLEDGEMENT

The senior author is grateful to the Department of Education at Northeastern University for providing office facilities during part of this study.

5

Tenacity in a Non-Caring Environment: Growing Up with Chemical Dependency and Sexual Child Abuse

Margo J. Heydt
Xavier University

These poignant childhood stories present the dynamics of neglect and abuse in the lives of five adult women. Participants' descriptions reveal that levels of neglect and emotional, physical, and sexual abuse were extremely high throughout their childhoods. The role of schools in the lives of these women and their families reveals the paradox of tenacity in a kind of odd collusion between schools and abusive parents, and between schools and abused children. In some families, abusive parents cloak the horror or disarray of their lives as parents by tenaciously holding to rigid expectations regarding school attendance and schoolwork. Some abused children, if they can get to school and then figure out how to stay there, cling to school in order to find a kind of safe haven or normality. The schools are just there, once again, tenaciously neutral. For some of these women, that neutrality was a welcome safety zone.

—Editors

* * *

During my first year in junior high, when I was 12, I was already in a relationship with an older boy. He was 19. He had permission from my mother and the school to pick me up on my lunch hours and take me to lunch. After school he picked me

41

up. I was always with him. At the time, it was convenient—a way to escape. The relationship went on for over 4 years. I had no girlfriends, no friends, nothing; just him. The only time I had [for myself] was before school. After school, we went to his apartment. I had sex, cooked, cleaned the house, everything at 12. I'm not so sure about how I felt. I'm just now realizing how much I missed out on.

This chapter tells the stories of five adult women who experienced parental chemical dependency and some kind of sexual abuse as children. The role of schools in the lives of these families problematizes the relationship between tenacity and caring.

This was not a study conducted to investigate the issues of caring in schools or of the relationship of tenacity to the factor of caring. The modified life histories that resulted from this study, however, included information about the role of education and schools in the lives of five women as children growing up with chemical dependency and sexual child abuse in their lives. The data document the possible significance of the construct of tenacity in two ways: (a) the consequences of the lack of any tenacious relationships with a caring adult in neglectful and abusive childhoods, and (b) the consequences of the paradoxical presence of some helpful school related tenacity within basically non-caring or abusive relationships and/or dysfunctional environments.

SUMMARY OF THE STUDY

The major data-gathering tool used in this study (see Heydt, 1994) was 12 hours of open ended, semistructured, in-depth interviewing of participants, conducted in four sessions per individual of 3 hours each. The interviews were designed to explore family dynamics identified in the literature on chemical dependency and sexual child abuse. Participants were asked in each interview to describe a typical day growing up in their family: first, in general; then, growing up with chemical dependency; then, growing up with sexual child abuse; and, finally, what they wanted to add to any of their previous descriptions. Grounded theory analysis of the data resulted in vivid participant descriptions revealing levels of neglect and emotional, physical, and sexual abuse that were extremely high throughout their childhoods. In fact, in addition to abuse from adults, the only participant not reporting being the victim of child-on-child sibling abuse was the only participant not living with any siblings.

PARTICIPANTS

All five research participants were chemically dependent adult females in a residential treatment facility for chemically dependent women at the time of the interviews. To participate in the study, residents had to have had at least one chemically dependent parent as a child and had to have been sexually abused as a child on at least one occasion. The five voluntary participants ranged in age from 25 to 42 years old. Four identified their race as caucasian and one identified herself as African-American. Education levels of the participants at the time of the study included two GED graduates, a high school graduate, and two college graduates, one with an associate's degree and one with a master's degree. Stated occupations included a factory worker, a professional cook, a registered nurse, and a mental health counselor. The fifth woman stated her occupation to be that of a "recovering addict" but most of her income came from prostitution.

The participants identified some kind of chemical dependency as being present in two out of five biological mothers and five out of five biological fathers plus various step/adoptive parents. All of the participants were sexually abused by at least one male offender by the age of 5 or 6. Four of the five had more than one perpetrator. Three of the five were abused for more than 5 years with at least two of these three being abused by one offender or another for more than 10 years. Four of the five were abused at least weekly, while three of the five were abused almost daily resulting in a very high frequency of abuse incidents overall. As for informing a parent of the abuse, three of the five participants had one or more parents who caused, encouraged, or knew about the abuse. Therefore, although parental knowledge of the abuse may have existed, it was not a deterrent in these cases. Finally, regardless of whether the nature of their sexual abuse was particularly violent, the data showed considerable evidence that the participants were surrounded by violence of all kinds in their lives.

None of the main sexual abusers of Teresa or Sharon[1] were people with whom the participant had a close, long-term, dependent relationship. It is likely that both of these participants had some part of their sexual abuse occur in or near a school or with some kind of reference to school. Neither of these participants had families who appeared to highly value education nor did either participant graduate from high school.

The other three participants all had close, long-term, dependent relationships with their main abusers. Violet, Sylvia, and Denise experienced abuse from the same abuser with whom they lived or practically lived over a period of 3 to 10 years. There were no indications that any reference to school was involved in the abuse of these three and, in fact, two of them specifically talked about school as being a better place than home. All three of these participants did well in school, had families in which at least one parent valued education, and graduated high school or higher education.

The following section describes the lives of these five participants primarily in their own words. Each description concludes with their reactions to school and the role of school in their lives (see Table 5.1 for summary data).

---

[1]These and all other names used in this chapter are pseudonyms.

Table 5.1. Continuums of School Related Data.

Continuums	Participants				
	Teresa	Sharon	Violet	Sylvia	Denise
Highest grade level achieved in school	Kicked out of school three times by Grade 8	Dropped out during 11th grade due to nervous breakdown	Graduated high school 1 year early	Graduated high school; associate's degree	Graduated high school; bachelor's and master's degrees
Participants' enjoyment of school	Hated school	Initially loved school, then hated it	Liked school "to get out of the house"	Loved school, "had all my fun there"	Loved school
Participants' involvement in school	No mention of grades or anything about homework	Poor grades, difficulty with homework; head injury	Good grades, "homework a must"	National Honor Society; beatings if not straight As; homework checked daily and done before allowed to play outside	Good grades with minimal effort; homework before TV
Family support of involvement in school	No mention of school activities	Wanted parents to attend school activities, but they wouldn't/ couldn't	Good at and enjoyed basketball, but abuser forbade practice after school	Made cheerleading squad, but abuser forbade participation	Participation in anything she wanted; many activities

Table 5.1. Continuums of School Related Data (cont'd).

Continuums	Teresa	Sharon	Participants — Violet	Sylvia	Denise
Family involvement in school	Biclogical father not involved; revolving door "stepfathers"; mother only required school attendance to avoid legal trouble	Biological parents only focused on attendance to avoid legal trouble due to homelessness	Biological mother enforced strict rules about homework and curfews, but not boyfriends; little relationship with stepfather; biological father would not insist on attendance	Biological mother not involved; biological father enforced rules with beatings; stepmother helped with homework and checked it	Both biological parents helped children with homework and encouraged educational values
School as a safe place	No memory of first grade; vomited daily to be sent home	Abuser "played school"; hungry; ridiculed due to poor clothes	Abuser picked her up from school twice daily; felt "out of place"	Father's behavior occasionally intruded with peers	Even abuser safe to be around in school

RESEARCH PARTICIPANTS AS CHILDREN

Teresa

Teresa was the youngest of six children born to her alcoholic and prescription drug addicted mother, who had six legal marriages and numerous live-in relationships. Teresa was born during her mother's fifth marriage. Her biological father was never a part of her life. Teresa's youngest half-brother was less than 1 year older than she and her middle half-brother was 3 years older than she. There were also three older half-siblings who were 10 or more years older than the oldest of these younger three, but they were not in the picture as much for Teresa growing up. She had several different home-life situations.

When Teresa's family lived in the south and she was probably about 4 or 5 years old, her older half-sister stopped babysitting for her and her two half-brothers. Her mother then started having the three of them put on their pajamas, take their radio, get in the car, and sleep in it while she was working and/or drinking in a bar. They were supposed to keep the doors locked and stay in the car. If one of them had to go to the bathroom, they would blow the car horn and their mother's friend would come out to get them. Sometimes, the children would go inside the bar, but Teresa recalled that watching her mother go-go dance was "*gross*." She remembered that her brothers would be drinking alcohol and smoking cigarettes in the car.

From growing up with her youngest half-brother, Teresa described learning that you need to be "cold" and not let someone know when something gets to you, in order to survive. Teresa reported that if she had a special doll, her youngest half-brother would burn it. If she wanted to watch a special television program, he would turn it off. If she turned it back on, he would hit or slam or punch her. Eventually, his abuse of her resulted in Teresa getting her own television and stereo for her room. Teresa reported that this same brother tried to kill her several times. She recalled two incidents with choking and another time he chased her around the block with a butcher knife when she was 9 months pregnant. Teresa also reported that her middle half brother saved her from one of the chokings by hitting the youngest brother until he came back to reality.

After the family moved north, but before the summer she was sexually abused, Teresa described 2 years during which her mother was physically ill with cancer and a heart attack. Teresa would have been about 7 and 8. In addition to drinking alcohol during that time, Teresa vividly recalled her mother laying on the couch with 25 pill bottles lined up on the coffee table and in the cabinet a pill bag containing 100 different kinds of pills.

It was during this 2-year period that the family ended up living in another trailer behind a bar. The drunks from the bar, who Teresa called the "*bar people*," began to come knocking. Teresa stated that she did not want the bar people coming in, but she did admit that she and her brothers liked robbing them after they passed out.

When the bar would close, my mom would bring everybody in the bar to the house. Everybody. I mean, everybody. . . . And we'd always keep our doors locked because them drunks always wanted to sleep on the floors or just mumbling, and grumbling, and throwing up everywhere . . . [we] would always be in the back bedroom by the time the whole bar came in. We were away in the back. We might as well watch TV. And always keep the door locked. But it never really bothered me. I knew they'd fall asleep sometime. I knew I was gonna take every bit of money I could get my hands on. I used to love it. There'd be people everywhere asleep, money falling out of their pockets. We'd see who could get the most money. They'd stay all night and sometimes all weekend. They'd get up and help Mom do the dishes and shit, you know, go to the store and get food for breakfast and my mom would cook breakfast. Do dishes again and then they'd all go out. Usually about 20 of them ended up staying, from the whole bar. Well, maybe 10. Twenty's an awful lot. And then they'd go out and a whole new batch would come in Saturday night. The batch from Friday night would go back over to the bar.

Teresa's history included many different incidents of sexual abuse with many different abusers, including her two half-brothers from ages 9 to 12. The abuser she felt was most damaging to her, however, was actually at least her fourth sexual encounter of some kind by the age of 9. This was a much older distant cousin to whom her mother sent her to live for the summer when she was 9 years old.

Teresa recalled being left there all summer, in a desolate rural area far from home, without any visits by her mother or any other family member. From her descriptions, this man spent incredible amounts of money and energy to procure and maintain an object for his sexual addiction, while he and his wife lived in a trailer with no indoor plumbing.

. . . every time he would do anything to me, then we would go and buy something. So at a young age, I learned about hustling. At a real young age . . . [he] instilled that sex for material things into my head. [He gave me a pony, go-cart, motorcycle, three-wheeler, new clothes, jewelry, little miniature diamonds, little small diamond rings and jewelry that I could never wear home. I had to leave this down there. High-heeled shoes . . . make-up, money. . . . He had a pony corral the first time I was down there. I said, "You got a pony?" He said, "No, but we'll sure get one for you." . . . So they bought me a pony. . . . They didn't have plumbing out there. They had an outhouse. And then there was a pond. And he bought me a boat to put in the pond and had them make me a trail. Hired somebody to make me a trail through the woods because he had like 15, 16 acres or something. And had a trail all the way back to the mountains and stuff for me to ride my bike, my three-wheeler, and my pony. It was just sick. Just sick. . . . You just knew that you shouldn't tell nobody. . . . Because it didn't feel right. I knew it wasn't right. Because he didn't tell nobody so I figured I shouldn't tell nobody. And I knew if I did tell anybody, it would probably stop all my gifts and stuff would be gone. . . .

I found out because, like, every time I did something, he'd take me and buy me something new or give me money to put away. "Put that away for when you go home." I had like $150 when I went home. . . . If I'd a been charging, he'd a been broke. It wasn't bad. $150 for a kid my age, you know. It's still sick. I'd rather I had no money and knew nothing.

Teresa provided a detailed report of what a typical day was like living with sexual child abuse that summer when she was 9. The following is her account of just the mornings, during which she may have been molested four or five times before lunch.

We'd get up and we'd have to go get eggs because we never had them. And I think he made it a point not to ever have them . . . eggs or cream . . . every morning. It happened every single day. He would buy a dozen eggs and half gallon of cream. And he drank that shit all day long. He'd let me drive the car. And he would do things to me, like, on the way to get the eggs. And then right before we'd get to the house where we was getting the eggs, we'd trade places. And then, we'd do it on the way back. And then we'd eat breakfast. . . . And then we'd have to go feed the horse and it would happen out there. After breakfast while [abuser's wife] was doing dishes. Then we'd go visit the horse and feed the horse and it happened out [in the barn]. . . . Then we'd take a ride on the three-wheeler, out in the woods and it would happen out there. And he had this bin. This metal bin that he kept a blanket and lotion and all kinds of stuff in out in the woods. Way out in the woods. . . . Had a padlock on it. . . . And he kept blankets and a pillow and lotion and [paper towels] and stuff in there. . . . Then when I wanted to take a ride, we'd take a ride. And then he'd want to stop and we'd do it again. And then we'd be right in front of the trailer. In the pond. On the boat. He'd always have me sit with my back to [abuser's wife]. She was in the house so she couldn't see what we were doing. I always wore little skirts and shit. And then we'd eat lunch.

Teresa was able to say no and get herself out of there when the molestation escalated and began to physically hurt. After that, Teresa maintained that no amount of manipulation or persuasion from the abuser could get her to return to his farm.

And I never, ever told him no except for the last time I was there. Because I thought he was trying to hurt me. . . . The last time that I was there he tried to put it in. . . . I think he got a little bit in because I was like bleeding. So [abuser's wife] thought I started my period so she went and bought me napkins . . . [abuser's wife said], "It's your period. These things happen to little girls." But it didn't keep on bleeding. I didn't start my period until I was 11.

After that incident, Teresa said she told them she wanted to go home and the wife took her home: "*And then I never went back down there ever again. But they used to come up to try to get me to go down there with them. They used to come up about every weekend and I wouldn't go.*" Teresa reported that the abuser told her, "I'll just let your pony die until you can get down here to take care of it. " Eventually, her pony was sold: "*It was like he was trying to persuade me to come back.*" She also reported that she was allowed to take one motorcycle home with her, but she finally took a sledgehammer to it.

The amount of sexual abuse to which Teresa was subjected throughout her childhood and adulthood prompted me to ask her when she was not experiencing some kind of sexual abuse. Her response was before kindergarten and for 6 months in 1985 "*as far as I can remember.*"

Teresa described little or no parental concern about her school grades or attendance. In fact, there was not a single comment about homework or grades in her data. All the data referred to attendance issues. She threatened to vomit on the only adult who really tried to enforce that.

We was never made to get up ever, never. Except to go to school, unless I played sick, which I did a lot. I'd go to school and pass out in the bathroom or pass out back behind the bleachers or in the woods. Or just skip school altogether and tell Mom, "I ain't going to school. I don't feel like it. I'm sick." She'd call the school, "Teresa says she don't feel like coming today, God damn it." The principal used to come and try to get me to go to school. And I'd say, "I'm not going. Get out of here. I'm gonna throw up right on you if you don't leave." "Been drinking, Teresa?" "No, I ain't been drinking. Get out of here. You're not my dad. You're just the principal of the school. And I'm not in school, so leave." I mean you could tell I was hung over, puking all night and shit.

Teresa emphasized her dislike of school in another interview:

They would try to get me out of bed. I would say I was sick, had a headache, tummy ache, something. I never wanted to go to school. Never, ever. They'd get me up. I'd miss the bus. Everybody in the house would be trying to get me up. I wouldn't want to get up. I hated school. I hated everything. I hated to sit still in one classroom and listen to one teacher. I just couldn't stand it. I thought education was just bullshit. I let them all know. I told Mom that, too. She'd say, "Well, it may be bullshit, but you got to go." Then they'd take me to school. Usually my mom would drop me off. Then 3 hours later, I'd be in the bathroom. I had thrown up. I learned that you had to throw up where they could see it. So I'd go walking down the hallway and put my finger down my throat and start puking all down the hall. And they'd say, "You need to come get Teresa because she's sick." Did this every day. That's why they kicked me out of school. Because I was not participating, I was unruly, I was wild, I was obnoxious, I was disrespectful. I just didn't want to be there. [But] only after [sexual abuse summer when we were living] in [the] north. After about fourth grade. Before then I went and bitched about it but I wasn't really unruly. But then I got so I was hitting teachers. I don't remember first grade. I remember kindergarten but I don't remember first grade in [the south]. Nothing. Sometimes I think I didn't go but I know I did but I don't remember anything about it. Not one single, not the kids, not the teachers, nothing. I don't know why. I'm scared to find out why because now I've heard you block out times in your life when something bad really happened. I don't know what could have happened. I just don't remember. . . . I remember the summer before. But I don't remember anything about that year. It's scary, really. . . . [In the north after the school called to say I was sick, Mom would] come get me at school. Then [I'd] come home and kick back and watch the soap operas, wait for everybody to get home from school. At my aunt's house. [mother's sixth husband] and my mother would be sitting in the kitchen drinking coffee and talking. . . . They wouldn't be drinking until 12. Home before noon. That's why I always ate breakfast. Had to have something to throw up. Wait for everyone to come home from school.

Although she described herself as always disliking school, Teresa noted a significant difference in her reaction to school after her summer of sexual child abuse: "I wasn't a hyperactive child until after all this abuse started."

I had been on Ritalin. School counselor referred me to a doctor who put me on Ritalin. When they took me off of Ritalin I put myself on speed to compensate for what they took from me. They say the Ritalin calmed me down but I remember it working in reverse on me. It's real abnormal for a female to be hyperactive. They said they could tell when I was growing out of it when the pills started working in reverse. But I never told them when they started working in reverse. It was like 6 months until they figured out.

Teresa also described having verbalized goals as a child that no one discouraged and for which she needed no formal schooling. She successfully reached all three stated goals by the time she was 16 or 17 years old.

Everybody thought it was funny that them were my goals: wanting to be a junky, a hooker, and a teenage mom. They thought that was funny but I was real serious. . . . My teachers thought I was insane. Miss [name] said, "Honey, I'll pray for you." She thought that would fix everything. She never even thought to attack the problems, that this kid really needs some help. Them were her only goals in life. That's why no one was surprised when Teresa went to the [prostitution hotel] or when Teresa was a junky or when Teresa got pregnant when she was 13. . . . My first pregnancy, I was happy because I felt like I had finally gotten somewhere. I was finally there. I didn't know where. But I felt important. I was going to school. I quit, though. They made me quit. I was in eighth grade and they said it wasn't appropriate for an eighth-grade kid to be walking around with this belly, you know. They asked me to quit. And then after, I went back and they asked me to quit because I was talking about birth control and it was inappropriate conversation.

When I asked Teresa how she thought things would have been for her if she had just grown up with chemical dependency and not sexual child abuse, she answered:

Then I would have been a drunk and not an addict. . . . I just think I would have been a drunk. I would have been a sloppy, fishy, drunk at 25. I would have had alcoholic paralysis or something. I would have drank as much as I do drugs. Because for me, alcohol didn't do it enough. . . . [Didn't] take the numbness and make me a different person than what I was. Drugs made me into a new person. When I started doing drugs, I became a dope fiend. I wasn't Teresa no more. I was Tiny, the dope fiend. And I could make up any kind of life I wanted to make up. Because nobody knew who I was, you know, so. . . . [Without the sexual abuse] I wouldn't need to be a new person. I could be just the way I was. . . . Yeah, if I wouldn't have been sexually abused, I could have finished school. I could have maybe went to college and been a normal alcoholic. Become an alcoholic in college, you know.

Sharon

Sharon's family lived in poverty most of her life due in part to her father's alcoholism, gambling, and sporadic employment. Her mother could not drive and only occasionally worked cleaning houses depending on where they lived. Sharon had a brother about 2 years older who died before she was born. Sharon remembered being told many times that she was supposed to have been a boy. Sharon's sister, who was 4 years older, physically and emotionally withdrew from Sharon all of her life. Apparently, Sharon was pushed out of a moving car by her sister at the age of 6. As a result, Sharon was in a coma for months and almost died.

For the first ten years of her life, Sharon remembers being hungry and homeless frequently:

I tell you, we moved so much. I never knew what home was. I never could get adjusted to friends or schools. We were always moving. We'd stay some place and wouldn't be able to pay the rent. And they'd throw us out. Move in with relatives. They'd get tired of us. We'd find another place to live. . . . If we didn't move, we wouldn't survive, plain and simple. That was exactly what it was all about. If we didn't move, we would die. . . . As an adult, I see back why we moved so much, because there was no food, there was no heat, there was no place to live and if we didn't go somewhere else, we would die. Plain and simple. When we were little, I was really withdrawn because of so much going on. I can remember looking back on myself. My depression that I suffered from a lot did not just start in my adult life. I remember as a child being absolutely totally depressed. . . . [I remember the] loneliness, overwhelmed by just life itself. Sad. I think even as a child I probably understood that. Because we didn't have nothing to eat.

Sharon vividly recalled many instances of having no food and being hungry all day. One memory included olfactory hallucinations of smelling food cooking:

I can remember one time when I was small. We lived out in the country. We never had no heat, in the dead of winter. Never had nothing to eat for days. And we stayed in that bed to stay warm, covered up. I can remember something smelled like it was cooking in the kitchen but we weren't cooking anything because there wasn't nothing. And Mom had gone over to the window to look out and she noticed her sweet potato vine growing. If you put a sweet potato in water it'll vine up. She had one growing in the window. And she noticed it and she cut the vines off and she sliced that sweet potato up and was frying it in some grease that she had. I remember setting down at the table. My sister and me took a piece. My mom took a little. My dad ate the rest of what was there. No human being needs to go through that.

Some of her father's more common practical jokes were also associated with food. Because the family rarely had money for things like soda pop, having one was considered special. When Sharon or her sister would be drinking one, their father would ask to have just a sip. Then he would drink the whole thing and laugh when he handed them back the empty bottle. The following is one of Sharon's more painful memories of her father's cruel and frequent practical jokes:

My dad had a sick sense of humor. I can remember back when we were very small. It may not mean a lot to somebody but it was to me and my sister. We had never had candy. I think I was 4 and my sister was 7. We went [to grandparents]. And Mom had worked to buy us some candy Easter eggs. And [my sister and I] went in the house. We were in there [searching] forever. And we come out and Daddy sat there and laughed. He was just laughing, I mean really laughing. And Mom says, "You shouldn't have done that." And we hunted and hunted and hunted. And there never was an Easter egg. He had sat there and eaten them all. And he thought that was real funny. I mean, that could be devastating to a little child. Doing something like that. But he would do stuff like that and he really thought it was hilarious.

Sharon reported it was a "common thing" for her father to come home from the bars covered with blood from fighting. Her father frequently brought home strangers he befriended at the bar to "sleep it off." Sharon remembered being frightened by having a stranger stay in their home overnight. Her sister would lock her bedroom door but Sharon's room did not have a door.

When her father would try to quit drinking, the family would usually attend church until he started drinking again. The sexual abuser that Sharon remembers was a young, homeless adult male stranger from their church who was staying with them for a while when she was 5 years old. Sharon reported pieces of memories of the sexual child abuse coming back to her over the year or two prior to the interview. She feels very unsure about how much more there is to remember. Sharon also stated that she could not recall how many times it happened with the one abuser she remembers, or if there were other abusers.

Her memory was of being 5 years old and the male stranger who was temporarily living with their family was babysitting her. Sharon remembered playing school with him and sitting on his lap while he was babysitting for her. Her next memory is of her parents coming home after she had been molested: *"They were smiling and this guy was smiling . . . just like everything was okay . . . no problem, everything's okay."* She recalled the family and the abuser sitting at the dinner table that evening and her father asking her why she was being so quiet because *"that wasn't like me, being real quiet."* But the abuser was at the table so she did not tell. Sharon was sure he had threatened her not to tell *"because I was really afraid"*, although she was not clear about the nature of the threat.

As for school fitting into her family's life, like Teresa, Sharon described a family that only complied with school attendance because it was law. . . . *"If it was school time, Mom always enrolled us. I remember her saying the law will get her if she don't. . . . Mostly moving around in the same area but different school districts because I remember changing schools all the time. . . . All different schools and different towns."*

Sharon's description of a typical day growing up in her family included several comments about what school was like for her:

The majority of the time, at that age, we really didn't have anything [to eat for breakfast], but when we did she would fix it. We'd go to school on the bus. 6:20. I really hated school. It wasn't the work; it was the kids. It was a bad time in school. They always made fun of me. My sister went through the same thing, too. Making fun of us for our clothes. They weren't that good. Had about two outfits and had to wear the same thing. I used to go down the hall and get real close to the wall so no one would notice me. My sister was so determined to not stay the way she was raised so she worked real hard in school. I would stay up all night to get it in my head. Sister got great grades and I didn't all through school. She graduated and I didn't. No friends or activities. I can remember going through the day starving to death. No breakfast and no lunch and getting home and still no food. That went on for years.

I never wanted to go to school. I did quit school. I had a breakdown at 16. . . . I just fell apart. All the pressure from all the years, I guess. The misery. Going to school and being made fun of. It was just a lot of things. I just broke. . . . I don't remember. I know I went to the doctor. He took me out of school. I can remember days. One day he knocked me out [with medication]. I just shook so bad. It was like I was in shock. I got suicidal. You know, maybe I wasn't beat up as a child. But I think of all the mental abuse. One thing that used to really hurt me was my mom and dad never attended school activities. Neither one of them. Just wouldn't go. If we had to have something to wear, she would iron it for us and help us to get ready, but she didn't go.

Violet

Violet was the middle child of three born in 4 years to her middle-class biological parents. They were divorced when she was 4 years old. Violet's contact with her father was severely restricted for a few years and then cut off completely for several years until she was about 14 or 15. At that time, she went to live with him, her stepmother, and their daughter. During the intervening years, Violet lived with her mother, stepfather, and maternal grandparents. Her grandmother was blind and both the stepfather and grandfather were alcoholics.

Violet described her mother as being the main rule setter in the home. Violet had to check in with someone at home after school; she was not allowed to do any chores because her grandmother would just re-do them; she was not allowed to go over to someone's home or have someone over to her house because "you don't know those people"; and she had to maintain a 10 p.m. curfew even when she was practically living with her older "boyfriend." The other rule that Violet described as being very important in her family was "keeping secrets."

Although she was only 1 year older, Violet's sister was 60 to 80 pounds heavier than Violet. Her sister was jealous of her and took out her violent temper on Violet. When her sister would begin to physically fight with Violet, their mother would enforce her rule of having to fight back by having the two of them go outside in the yard and wrestle each other. When her sister ripped out her hair and held a butcher knife to her throat, Violet called the authorities herself. As they got older, Violet's younger brother became her protector. He would fist fight the older sister to keep her from fighting Violet; he would have to "knock her simple."

Although her biological father was an alcoholic, most of Violet's experiences with alcoholism as she was growing up involved her maternal grandfather and her stepfather. She recalls all chemical use being forbidden in the house except by her stepfather. Every day after work, he would drink a case of beer while he was watching television, then stop at a certain time and go to bed. Violet stated that her only relationship with her stepfather was getting his beer. When her mother brought it home, it was Violet's chore to put the beer in the fridge like they did the soda with the cold ones in front and the warmer ones in back. Then while he was drinking she was to give him his beers and take away the empty bottles.

Violet used to "rush" to take the empties away because there always would be some beer left in the bottles. Even though she hated the taste, she would hold her nose as she drink the leftover ale. She estimated that by drinking those leftovers she was probably drinking a couple of beers each night herself before she was in junior high school. During this same time period, Violet was also sneaking gallon bottles of vodka on a fairly regular basis to her grandfather because her mother and grandmother did not allow him to drink.

Violet was sexually molested first by her paternal step-grandfather. Violet recalled some details of the abuse from her grandfather when she was ages 5 or 6 through 8: "*I would have to sit there on his lap to see the [coin collection]*" but "*what sticks in my mind the most is him kissing me with his tongue in my mouth.*"

Violet's main abuser, however, was her first "boyfriend," arranged by her mother with a 19-year-old son of a friend of the family. This abusive, practically live-in relationship lasted for 4 years, starting when Violet was 12. For 2 or 3 years while Violet was in junior high school until he entered the military service, Violet's typical day with this boyfriend was described as follows:

He would pick me up at lunch. We went out to lunch. I smoked at that time so I had to be out of the school vicinity to smoke. He bought me cigarettes. We'd go somewhere to eat and he would take me back to school. We might have had oral sex or something. We went for a ride. . . . He'd be sitting right beside the school to pick me up [after school]. He lived clear on the other side of town. He was there everyday. He'd pick me up. Usually we went right straight to his house unless we stopped at the grocery or something But usually he did that. You know, the more I think about it, he would be drinking beer when he picked me up. . . . He rented an apartment, not with other family. We would go to his apartment. His mother came over a lot. She was aware of everything. It would be like an hour and a half after I would get there from school on her way home from work. She would visit a little bit. She knew I was 12 and in the seventh grade. I usually tried to do my homework in school. If I had homework, I would do it sometime that evening. The first thing we would do is go in the living room, watch TV, and have sex. Then I usually took my bath. Then I cooked dinner. While I was in the bath, he'd be watching TV. I always made dinner by myself. Then we would eat dinner together at the kitchen table. We talked. . . . Usually after

*dinner, I'd go talk to [neighbor family] on the porch. He'd watch TV or
something. I did the dishes right after we ate. He watched TV and maybe
rested some. This is when I'd do my homework if I had any. Usually we'd
sit in the living room for a while and watch TV and then he would take me
home. And I was there on time. I was still on a curfew time. He made sure I
was home by curfew. . . . I would instantly go up to my bedroom. I turned
on TV and lay down and would go to sleep. I was exhausted by then. I
remember really being tired. I never felt like I had enough sleep or rest.
And then I would get up the next morning and start all over. Usually my
clothes were picked out for me. All I had to do was follow the routine.*

From Violet's description, it appeared that she was literally handed over by the
mother to the boyfriend, who then controlled all her waking minutes except
when she was in class and for an hour before school every day. Her mother
never asked Violet what went on with him as long as the boyfriend got her back
home by curfew at 10 every night.

*I think she knew where I would be at all times so. I don't ever remember say-
ing I didn't want to go because I didn't want to stay home either. . . . I really
don't know why I feel like I didn't have any freedom at home or why I never
wanted to be there. I just really don't have all those answers [yet]. But it was
from one hell to another . . . if it hadn't been for my brother I would have
cracked. We would leave home as soon as we could and do everything we
could in that time. That was my childhood, right there in that hour every day
[before school], pitching quarters.*

During the summers, Violet was with her abuser almost 24 hours a day. She
labeled the abuse from this boyfriend as love for more than 20 years until she
was in the treatment program at the time of the interview. When I asked Violet
about that and about whether he set any rules for her, she answered:

*When he wanted sex, we did it. That was a lot. Every day, maybe more than
once. . . . I can remember quietly crying a lot when we would be having sex.
Tears would be coming but I wouldn't say anything. I don't think he
noticed. It hurt, but evidently that did not matter. I think I would have been
made to do it anyway if I had said no. He would have just picked me up and
carried me. . . . I can remember actually trying to fight sometimes, but I
think he liked that. I would try to fight him off and say no but he liked it.
After a while we would wrestle before sex, like a struggle sort of that was
supposed to be fun, like kids would play, I felt. Sometimes it would hurt,
too, exchanging punches [and] pinning me down. I got extremely mad a
couple times where I really wanted to hurt him, but I think he enjoyed that
when I got mad. Sex got to be a routine; never any feeling around it. I think
at that time I thought about other things. I was not there really. Physically,
I was; mentally, I wasn't. This was not lovemaking. He did say I love you a*

lot. Then I thought it was love. I thought I was never going to be with any-body else in my whole life. Now I know the wrestling was abuse. I didn't know that before. Oral sex was a must, everyday. That was usually before we would have vaginal sex. In the same event, I would have to do both. I would have to do oral sex a lot [sometimes] while riding in the car while he was driving.

When I first asked Violet what would be the three most important things to know about living in her family, she answered literally: *"Be home on time; brush your teeth; do your school work. Homework had to be done before we went anywhere."* Violet's comments about school showed that she attended school to get out of the house, succeeded in her schoolwork because she had to do her homework and because it came easy to her, but that she never felt a part of anything that happened at school.

I was good in school. I enjoyed school. I've been talking about it now on an individual basis with my counselor. I never made friends. I did what I had to do in school and nobody really knew me personally or my family person-ally. I got good grades. . . . I remember all my [elementary school] teach-ers. I was always good in school. Didn't have trouble with grades. Didn't put a lot into it. It came easy to me. I skipped school [only] one time in high school. I really liked school. I liked getting out of the house. By high school, I just did what I had to do to graduate. . . . I usually tried to finish my homework at school. If I had some, I would have to do it as soon as I walked in. Right after school, "while your mind's still fresh." [It was] Mom's rule.

Violet's comments about school once she reached junior high school included her activities before and after school, which were very important to her.

I was real close to my brother. We would pitch quarters. We would hang out at the laundry mat. I hung out with a lot of boys. . . . You pitch quarters to see who can get it closer to a mark you're shooting at and that person gets all the quarters. I was good at it. My brother was pretty good. I won a lot and always split my winnings with my brother. And we smoked so we needed money to buy cigarettes. I got in trouble after a while at school because I won everybody's lunch money and no one was eating. [The school] made the laundry mat off limits. . . . I remember wanting to get on the basketball team at school. I was really good at basketball. And, of course, you had to be there early before school, which I didn't want to give up that time. Or practice after school. And I had to miss out on playing bas-ketball during my 3 years in junior high. I missed out on that fun time and gave it up and [older boyfriend] wouldn't allow me to after school. It was like an hour and a half. [Older boyfriend] did make rules for me. I'm not sure if I made anyone else aware of it but he did. . . . I pretty much had asked permission from him for anything I did instead of my mother.

Later, after Violet was in high school and her boyfriend had entered the military, she moved in with her father and stepmother. Like Teresa and Sharon, Violet did not believe her father would have forced her to go to school. But like Sylvia and Denise, attendance, homework, and grades had been important enough while she lived with her mother that Violet apparently internalized those standards for herself.

> *I was still writing the boyfriend and I didn't really make friends in high school. I stayed close to home and worked and did dope. I didn't really make friends. But the longer he stayed away, . . . I guess I just kind of realized that wasn't what I really wanted. I kept telling Daddy. He said that was something I didn't have to do. I had no contact with Mom after I moved in with my father. She just really cut me off. No visitation. I don't even remember talking to her during those couple of years. Even graduation. I never got a graduation card or nothing. I didn't walk through commencement. I sent out the announcement and everything and never heard anything from Mom's side of the family. I'm going to ask her about that. That just really. She just always, you know, that was a must. You need your diploma. I really wouldn't have had to go to school after I went with Dad. I don't think he would have forced me to go if I really said I don't want to go to school. It was one thing I really wanted to.*

Besides her parents, Violet's "boyfriend" played an important role in her schooling. Although he forbid after school activities, he did nothing to directly interfere with her attendance or homework. In fact, Violet viewed him as keeping her safe during school in the turbulent 1960s. In her discussion of a typical day with her "boyfriend," Violet referred to what she perceived as her abuser's protector role of her at school. "During school then, there was a lot of racial things going on, a lot of drugs, Vietnam. And I was safe. You know what I mean? He made sure I was safe from all that, rioting and all that. He was my guardian angel."

Sylvia

Sylvia's biological parents were never married to each other and lived together for only a short time when Sylvia was an infant. Sylvia's biological mother was alcoholic and was married to someone else when Sylvia was conceived. Her biological father was addicted to drugs and alcohol and was a drug dealer for many years. As a toddler, Sylvia was legally adopted by a maternal great aunt and uncle. Her fond memories of living with them were cut short when the aunt sent her to live with her biological father after discovering her husband fondling Sylvia. She has no memory of this abuse, although she has many clear and vivid positive memories of her brief time with them as a preschooler.

Sylvia spent the rest of her growing up years living with her biological father and stepmother, who she considers to be her real mother. Both the father and stepmother were blue-collar workers who divorced when Sylvia was in her late teens. Although she had three half siblings from her biological mother, Sylvia grew up as an only child. When Sylvia would visit her biological mother and three siblings on weekends as a very young girl, her mother would leave the four youngsters alone and be gone overnight drinking. Sylvia described how it would be getting dark and there would be no food to eat; that her younger little sister would be crying because she was hungry and that she and her little brother would wet their beds; and that her older sister would be trying to feed all four of them by putting frozen food in her toy easy-bake oven. Finally, Sylvia would go to the neighbors and call her father and stepmother to come to get her. After a few such visits, she stopped visiting her mother.

Sylvia's life with her father and stepmother was completely controlled by her father. Some of her father's rules that Sylvia felt affected her the most included: coming home from school at an exact time no matter what the weather or bus schedule; not answering the phone or the door or going outside when home alone; not having friends, which included no bike riding with neighborhood kids, no overnights, no going downtown with her girlfriends, and no talking with boys; "stay in a child's place," which meant not expressing any opinions about adult behavior or business; and "if you disagree with me then you can get out".

Sylvia stated that she had to do what her father told her to do or he would cuss her out or hit her: "*I did what I was told because I was smacked in the mouth if I said no when I was a small child so I didn't say no very often.*" When Sylvia was little she would be spanked very hard with a belt or switch, sometimes dressed and sometimes not dressed. If her stepmother would try to interfere on her behalf, Sylvia's father would lock his wife out of the room while he spanked Sylvia.

On a typical school day, after having fun with her National Honor Society friends on the bus ride home from school, Sylvia would hurry to the house to be home on time. When she got home, her father would be there waiting for her: "*if I was okay on the time, he didn't say anything and I would just go right on in, put my books down, and start doing homework.*" If Sylvia got home from school just a minute or so late, "*I just got hollered at a whole lot.*" But if she were later than that, no matter what the reason, it would be considered a rule infraction. Sylvia's father gave her a serious physical beating about a couple of times a year for these rule infractions: "*he would add my beatings up . . . if I did something . . . a lot of times, 'you got one coming' . . . he would verbally abuse me on that and put a credit toward a whooping and once a credit got so far up, then he would beat me for everything.*"

When Sylvia was a young teenager, her father began drinking less and using drugs more while her stepmother began working evening shift. So he switched his chemical use and dealing activities to the house. She stated that her father always had somebody at the house as she got older. The phone would start ringing and people would be waiting for him to get home from work and then they started coming over to the house "*left and right.*" She said that some came for drugs; some came hoping for free drugs, and some came to play cards, sit, talk, and smoke marijuana. She also recalled that sometimes when she was about 16, her father would only have guys at the house and they would watch X-rated movies. At those times, Sylvia was forbidden to come downstairs to use the bathroom or to get any food without permission.

In addition to physical and emotional abuse, Sylvia's father also became her sexual abuser for 3 years when she became a teenager. She had a difficult time describing a typical day growing up with sexual child abuse:

> *You know, that's hard to answer because there was not a typical day. Because I wouldn't know what kind of a mood he would be in. It would just like happen, boom. All of a sudden. It wasn't anything that I can remember that was a typical day and then he would do it. It just happened. . . . He did the same things. Come home or watch TV or bring his friends over. They'd sit in the kitchen and do all drugs or what not or play cards. There wasn't anything specific. I couldn't even pinpoint when he would do it. I was always on pins and needles thinking, is this going to be the night or what? I would never know. So there was no set ritual.*

Sylvia pieced together a history of being raped between four and six times a month starting when she was 12 and ending when she was 15. It usually happened at night after all her father's friends were gone: "*anywhere between maybe 9:00 or so. Then I did know. It would be about that time when I was about ready to go to bed.*" But it did not happen after her stepmother got home from work at almost midnight: "*. . . then I knew I was safe.*" So for about 3 hours every night, Sylvia would wait to see if her father would come to rape her. "*I was always mentally wondering. You, know, because I couldn't ever tell when. So after a while you just normally worry about that.*"

Sylvia's reactions to her father were strictly negative and often related to his "*whorish*" sexual behavior in general as opposed to his sexual abuse of her specifically. After finding out he was sexually abusing or trying to abuse a neighbor at the same time that he was abusing Sylvia, she commented that he was "*like peanut butter, spreading hisself all over.*"

The family Sylvia described became an example of living an open secret after her first pregnancy. When Sylvia was 13 and pregnant for the first time, her step-grandmother to whom she was very close, thought it was from a boy. But Sylvia "*told her who did it and she said I made a mistake by what I said, and I said no, my father did this.*" The step-grandmother told Sylvia's stepmother, who confronted the father. He denied everything and threatened Sylvia. Sylvia maintained the truth, but no one removed her from the situation. Sylvia endured three pregnancies and her stepmother took her for three abortions in 2 years.

After 3 years of sexual abuse on top of the emotional and physical abuse, Sylvia described how the sexual abuse ended when she was 15:

He got sicker with that [physical abuse] as he got older and he was more into his own drug usage. He got sicker. Until one day, I blacked out or something. And when I came to, he was calling my name. I had a black tire hose wrapped around his neck and was squeezing real tight and his jugular veins were extending. Because I just wasn't gonna take no more beatings any more. Or any more sexual abuse. I was just sick of it. And there was plenty of times when I was planning on either running away or killing myself. And then I would say, "I'm not gonna do that and leave my [step-mother] with that man." So I'm just gonna have to do something because I'm not gonna take it anymore. I was ready to fight. . . . I thought he was gonna kill me after that. He got up and sat down. He got up and got on the couch and sat down. And told me to go upstairs and leave him alone. And I was so shocked by his reaction that I didn't know what to do because I just knew I was going to be killed, you know. But he left me alone and didn't touch me no more. In fact, he never bothered me anymore after that.

When asked about school, Sylvia stated: "*I had all my fun at school.*" She explained this to mean that she would "*joke around and really talk to my friends at school . . . and at lunch time act silly in the cafeteria and stuff . . . my class-mates would laugh at me and stuff . . . oh, just do something silly, you know, try to belong to the crowd.*" Sylvia denied acting silly in class because she feared getting in trouble with the teachers and then her father. She described her girl-friends as mostly "A" students like herself: "*We were on the honor society together.*" This group of four to six girls would sit together in class, eat lunch together, and some of them rode the bus together.

When I asked Sylvia what she liked best about school, she responded:

being with people . . . hat was the only time I really got to socialize . . . and be around people my age . . . that was my time . . . I looked forward to going to school and I did not ever want to miss a day of school . . . not even when I got sick . . . I had to beg my (step)mother to let me go to school because I didn't want to miss it . . . because I knew when I came home I wasn't going to be able to be around anybody . . . and that's what I looked forward to, was being around my friends.

Sylvia described many school-related rules from her father. Part of her typical day description included rules about homework.

After dinner I cleaned up the dishes. . . . And then I could go back out and play for whatever time was left before the sunset, provided I had my home-work done. And I had to bring my homework down and have it checked first. . . . My father didn't do no checking. [It was] my dad's rule and my mother did it. Plus she wanted to make sure I had my work done, too, before I went out. And she would help me with things I did not understand. Because I would play until the sun would set and then come in and get me a bath before I went to bed. . . . I was a good student but I was always preached to get straight As. I wasn't necessarily an A student. The only thing that kept me from being a straight A student was English. I was not a very good English person as far as composition. I'm real good in the comprehension part but the components of sentences. I just couldn't grasp that as well. And I come home with Bs and Cs in component English. Literature I came home with As in. He just couldn't understand why I couldn't get As and threatened to beat me if I didn't come home with As. And I tried and tried. And it would just get on my nerves to try and I couldn't do it, you know, very successful. And my mother, in many instances, stopped him from whooping me for my report card because she said, "Look at all these other grades. You can't be good in every subject." And he said I had to and I don't know why because he didn't even finish high school. But yet he had to be hard to me about my grades. And I couldn't miss any days of school. Better not be late for school and better not be late coming home from school. And I was riding the city bus . . . I told him I can't get home any faster than what the bus carries me. "Well, you better get off and run home then because you better have your ass in the door by 3:30."

Denise

Denise grew up in a traditional; upwardly mobile, intact middle-class family. Both parents were professionals in the community. Her father was a binge alcoholic. Her brother was 4 years older than she.

Denise's description of a general typical day growing up in her family could fit a traditional middle-class television family such as on programs like Leave it to Beaver or The Brady Bunch. She described both parents helping her brother and her to get ready for school in the mornings: "*we always had breakfast together in the morning.*" Denise walked to school with her older brother and came right home after school. She contrasted loving school, being good at it, and having lots of friends with her brother hating school, not being good at it, and having fewer friends: "*I always felt guilty about how good I was in school and how easy it was for me. It seemed like he really struggled; my Mom would spend like hours with him.*" She reported that her mother cooked dinner every night: "*we had to eat dinner at home; I mean that was forever, that was a rule, that was real important to my mom.*" After dinner, her mother and brother worked on his homework while Denise and her father watched television together. Then it would be time for bed. Denise commented that her mother "*made sure*" they had lots of family time together.

Denise's description of a typical day growing up with chemical dependency in her family was quite different. When her father came home after drinking, Denise and her brother would be quiet and on their best behaviors because their parents would be upset with each other. Their father would try to talk with their mother and make up. Their mother would be "icy," "withholding," like a "curtain dropped." The family would sit down to a "real chilly" dinner. Denise stated that she learned not to make her father angry when he was drinking. If her father only had a couple of drinks, he would act like a buddy to people. With more drinking, he expressed more anger and reacted more quickly with anger.

For a few years, he was able to go for several months at a time without drinking, but Denise stated that waiting for it to happen was worse than having it happen more frequently. Later when Denise was a teenager. he became more secretive about his drinking and would run the faucet in the kitchen, so no one could hear the popping sound of opening the beer can, and would down a beer in 20 seconds. The family could count how many beers he had by how often he ran the water.

Denise emphasized how normal the daytime was of her typical day growing up with sexual child abuse. She described enjoying her brother in the daytime, especially when they would play with other kids in the neighborhood. But when it got dark and bedtime was coming, Denise would "start getting scared." When Denise was about 5 or 6 years old, her brother began "tormenting" and "terrorizing" her on a daily basis by doing such things as climbing out his bedroom window and making faces and noises outside her bedroom window: "I never knew what to expect. . . . It never felt safe."

Sometimes when Denise opened her closet, her brother would be hanging upside down in the closet with fangs in his mouth and a flashlight on his face. When Denise would complain to her parents, her father insisted that this was what all older brothers do to their younger sisters, and her mother agreed. Her parents would tell her brother to stop, but they would do nothing when he persisted. One time when Denise was 8, he locked her in the coal bin in the cellar for an hour without any light: "I think he terrorized me . . . like a hostage situation."

The "teasing" and "tormenting" at bedtime was going on all the time beginning at age 5. After age 7, the abuse escalated. It started with the tormenting after dark and then Denise would become "vigilant and [be] waiting for something to happen"; she would be laying there listening to every noise in the hallway and "waiting for the doorknob to turn and for him to come in"; she would be "praying he wouldn't come." Her brother would "come in and touch me" on the arm or leg or back. Denise would wake up, say his name, and he would leave. After he left her room, "he never came back" so then she would feel safe. Denise just considered it a part of the tormenting at the time because in the beginning, the only difference was that he was only touching her and not scaring her: "he'd just laugh or something and leave the room." It was happening two or three times a week on and off from age 7 to 12.

Then when her brother got old enough, about 12 or 13, he would babysit for Denise when their parents were away. This began when she was 8 or 9:

> If they would leave to go out to dinner, I would like just scream. Blood-curdling, horrible. I can remember standing at the front door screaming at the top of my lungs, "Don't leave." And so [they said] I was kind of being self-centered and selfish. I was saying "don't leave me because he's hurting me." And I complained a lot about him because he also tormented me. A lot. But then it was kind of written off as all older brothers do that. They terrorize their younger sisters.

Denise reported that her brother never specifically threatened her verbally or physically:

> except for that one time. Where he actually, in the middle of the daytime, threw me on the ground. . . . And my mom and dad were gone somewhere. . . . And he started like grabbing at me, like up here [chest]. And this was like the middle of the afternoon. And I pushed him away. And he threw me down on to the kitchen floor and ripped my shirt off. And I just screamed at the top of my lungs. And he stopped and he ran out of the house. . . . I couldn't pretend it wasn't happening. . . . But this time it was like he lost his mind. He wasn't himself. And it was obvious what he was going to do to me. . . . I said, "Stop it" or something And he said, "I can do anything I want to you" or something.

Denise gave a clear description of what the sexual abuse was like when she got a little older:

> Like I can remember, like, the first time I really knew something was wrong And that was, like, when I was 12. Because at that time, when we moved to the other house. . . . They had this house built and it had locks on the doors. And I can remember being glad about that. . . . That's what I can remember the most vividly . . . and being 12 and up. And he was 16. Right. Because at that time then he started doing things like. I'd wake up and he'd have his face between my legs. Or he took my hand and put it on his penis. I'd wake up and he'd have my hand touching him and like rubbing it. . . . And there were a lot of times when there would be. Like I'd be awake. I didn't want to have it out. I didn't want to. I was so ashamed and humiliated. I didn 't want to look at him and say what are you doing or why are you. It was just too humiliating So I'd cough or roll over just to signal him that I'm awake and it was not okay. And he would leave. Sometimes he'd leave and sometimes he'd stay. I guess thinking, she'll fall asleep. Or I'll just wait here until she. Because I could hear him breathing And then I would just lay awake. And then he would think I was asleep and then would start to do something And then I'd say, "Get out of here." And then I would say something to him. It was like I was trying to get him to get out and stop without

having to say anything to him about it. But at that point, there were a lot of times when I would say, "Leave me alone. " I'd cry, you know, "Please, get out of here." . . . He'd say, "I'm sorry" and he'd leave. He was never, like. He never said things to me like, if you don't let me do this I'm gonna hurt you. Or, you know what I mean. He was never threatening or. But he would be real sad like. . . . It was just like, just ongoing. Like all the time. And I started locking my door. . . . I don't remember a night going by that it didn't happen.... And he would unlock the door. And that would wake me up sometimes. I'd hear the click and I'd say, "Stay out of here." And he'd leave. But other times it didn't wake me. [It ended when] He went away. When he graduated from high school. . . . So I was 16.

Denise felt that her mother's role in the sexual abuse was more clear than was that of her father. She thought it would kill her mother to know that her brother was abusing her because her mother was "*crazy about my brother*": "*she always had explanations for all the trouble he got into . . . his whole life . . . year after year after year . . . no matter what he does.*" But Denise could not recall her mother making excuses for her brother's tormenting of her: "*that's where my dad might have come in.*" Denise was able to identify that her father's drinking played a role in the sexual abuse continuing when she was older because telling him would have been one more problem: "*one more thing to upset him . . . one more reason he didn't want kids.*" Although Denise viewed her brother as being her mother's favorite, she saw herself as her father's favorite and was afraid that if she told about the abuse she would no longer be his favorite.

For Denise, school was not a problem area of her life. It was totally separate from the many problems at home.

Oh, I loved school. I loved it a lot. My brother hated it. He wasn't very good at school. I liked it a lot. I was good at it. I always had a lot of friends. He didn't have very many. He had a few. . . . Reading was so hard for him. I can remember coming home from school and not wanting to show my report card on the same day he got his because I'd have all As and he would have flunked two or three things. . . . I didn't do much homework. I really didn't. I would do it at school or on the way home or bullshit my way through it somehow. In high school, I never took a book home. I did it all in study halls. I'd come home from school and Mom would be home. When Mom and Grandpa bought this store, then he'd work and she'd make sure she was home a lot of the time. And she'd cook dinner for us. Then we sat in front of the TV unless we weren't done with our homework.

Denise repeated this theme about school several times. She did not have many comments about school that differed from that positive experience.

Since my, mom and I started talking about the incest and stuff like that, we've taken a look at a lot of stuff that happened back then. I really seemed

so well adjusted. I mean, I really did. People just didn't think I needed any-
thing like [praise or extra attention]. I had a lot of friends, took tap danc-
ing, ballet, piano lessons, got good grades. It seemed like I didn't need that
much attention.

DISCUSSION

No matter what their racial, ethnic, cultural, or socioeconomic backgrounds, all
five of these girls had so much neglect and abuse in their lives that it is a wonder they physically survived to adulthood, much less paid attention to anything
at school. As children, their common denominators were living with abuse and
addictions. As adults, these women's experiences included even more common
ground: many abusive relationships, unplanned pregnancies, periods of losing
custody of their children, drug and alcohol addictions in themselves and their
partners, and three of the five spent considerable time in jail, including the one
who later got her master's degree. Attitudes toward and success in attaining an
education is one of the few areas in which these women differed greatly as children and adults. Their experiences help explicate the paradoxical place of caring
as tenacity in terms of being able or not being able to persevere at doing school.

Along with their families, the five participants' experiences with
schooling can be placed along three parallel continua:

1. From the earliest drop out date to the highest degree attained.
2. From the least enjoyment and least family involvement to the most
    enjoyment and most family involvement.
3. Feelings about school as a safe place.

Two of the participants reported not liking school, not being good at it,
and not graduating high school, while three of the participants reported being
good in school, liking it, and graduating high school. The participant who disliked
school the most and had the least family support for or involvement in her education and school-related activities was also the one who dropped out in the earliest
grade—eighth grade. The participant who loved school and had the most family
support for and involvement in her education and school-related activities
obtained the highest level of education of the five—a master's degree. On the continuum of education completed, the places of the other three participants correlate
to the continua of feelings about school as a safe place and of family emphasis on
and participation in the participant's education no matter what neglect, abuse, dys-
function, or addiction was happening in other aspects of their lives.

For Teresa and Sharon, little about school seemed positive or safe.
Teresa *"hated"* school, thought of education as *"bullshit,"* never wanted to go,
and would fake being sick to stay home or get sent home. She was *"kicked out"*

of school at least three times before her final departure in eighth grade. The next participant on these continua, Sharon, started out loving school but kept changing schools all the time and then was "*hungry, tired, and had no clothes so I didn't want to go.*" She reported having no friends, not involved in activities, and "*hugging the wall to not be noticed.*" Her doctor took her out of school at the beginning of Grade 11 due to her "*nervous breakdown*" and she never went back.

Teresa was very troubled by her lack of any memory for an entire grade at school. Although she does not remember whatever emotional, physical, and/or sexual abuse likely happened during first grade, more than once she gave responses indicating that she was never really a kid "*except maybe before kindergarten*" and that the only time in her life without abuse was before kindergarten. Teresa described disliking school prior to her summer of sexual abuse but then hating it after that. Teresa never reported having problems with any particular teachers or peers. Just believing school was "*bullshit*" does not seem to be a serious enough problem to warrant a fifth grader making herself vomit on a daily basis in order to get out of school, especially because all she did when she escaped school was watch soap operas at home until her friends got out of school.

Sharon's memory of sexual abuse included "*playing school*" with her abuser. In addition, school was a place where one was made fun of for not having good clothing. This ridicule was severe enough to cause Sharon to try to disappear into the walls of the hallway so no one would notice her. And school was no better than home for someone who was hungry all day. The possible effects of her head injury, from being pushed out of the car by her sister at age 6, on her ability to succeed at schoolwork also need to be considered and appear not to have been evaluated. She never mentioned missing first grade or being a year older than her peers, both of which would seem to have been likely. Although Sharon spoke about having two different years in her life for which she had no memory (ages 6 and 16), she never mentioned how this affected school except that ultimately she never went back. Like Teresa, it appeared that nothing about school felt positive or safe for Sharon either.

For the other three participants who graduated, high school was a more positive and safe place, or at least was perceived as being safer than home. Violet, the middle participant on these continua, got good grades and liked school because she "*liked getting out of the house.*" She reported not socializing in school, not having friends in school, and not participating in school activities. Violet felt like she "*didn't fit in*" because "*nobody knew me*" and "*I already knew about and was having sex when we learned about it in health class.*" In a time when students were not allowed to leave school at lunchtime, the school was given permission by Violet's mother to allow the boyfriend to take this seventh and eighth grader out of school for lunch every day. He was also waiting for her right after school every day: "*The only time I had [for myself] was before school.*" Violet did talk about being very interested in and good at basketball in junior high and very much wanting to be on the school team. But her older boyfriend did not allow it after school and her own need to have that 1 hour of childhood a day with her brother was more important before school. In addition, with external school factors such as drugs, war, and racial conflicts, neither home nor school felt safe to Violet as she got older. Turning to her abuser to be her "*guardian angel*" felt like the safest alternative available to her. Despite all this, graduating was a goal of hers and she continued to do her homework after being raped at the boyfriend's apartment, doing well enough to graduate ahead of her class, at the end of her junior year. Because she had chosen to live with her father for a couple of years as a teenager, however, this girl's mother, who had insisted on homework and graduation, refused to attend her graduation.

The last two participants on these continua both excelled in school grades and had at least some involvement in school activities. Sylvia reported having all her fun in school, loved being with people, and would sometimes play the class clown in order to belong to the crowd. She and her closest girlfriends were all in the honor society. She even tried out for cheerleading and made the squad but her father forbade her from participating. She was not allowed to participate in any after school activities. Both Violet and Sylvia wanted to participate in school activities but were not allowed to by their abusers. Sylvia's social life at home was restricted as was Violet's: No friends allowed. But rather than withdrawing like Violet did, school felt safe and positive and became Sylvia's social outlet.

Violet's sexual abuse may have become associated in some way with school because that was where her abuser came to get her twice a day, every school day for years. Sylvia's sexual abuse only directly intruded into her schooling at times when her father's reputation with drugs and/or sex became known. On one occasion, she described having a classmate tell how Sylvia's father tried to "*hit on*" her at her birthday party, a party that Sylvia was not allowed to attend. Sylvia told her mother and, after they confronted her father, he admitted being at the high school girl's party.

Both Sylvia and Denise loved school and did very well in it. Both were safe from the abuse at home when they were in school. Denise's brother never bothered her in any way when other kids were around so that even her brother was safe to be around when they were at school. Denise described loving school, making good grades with minimal effort, having lots of friends, and participating in as many activities as she wanted. In addition to graduating high school, Sylvia completed an associates' degree and Denise completed both a bachelor's and then a master's degree as an older adult student.

CONCLUSIONS

These five girls were surrounded by addicts who reserved their caring for their addictions or by partners of addicts who maintained their primary caring for the addict. No matter what the appearance to others, the basic emotional needs and often physical needs of these children did not come first for anyone, including school officials.

For Teresa and Sharon especially, there appeared to be almost a total lack of any tenacity on anyone's part regarding their schooling or education. Both knew the difference between being sent to school by parents to avoid legal trouble for themselves and being sent to school because of parental interest or caring about the child getting an education.

Both Sharon and Teresa's families barely met the minimum legal requirements of schooling. Teresa's mother and other family members persisted in trying to get her out of bed to go to school. *"We was never made to get up ever, never. Except to go to school . . ."* When she missed the bus, they drove her there, or called the school to report her illness when she was just too sick from alcohol consumption to get out of bed. With each move in search of shelter and food, Sharon's mother enrolled both her daughters in the new school. She saw to it that they were on the bus at 6:20 a.m. She would try to iron their meager clothing when they were expected at school for a special activity, although neither she nor the girls' abusive father ever attended.

The school responded in kind, dealing only with the students, per se, and not with the chaos of their lives at home. Teresa was disruptive, and that was the behavior symptom that the school noted. From the principal, the truant fourth grader heard, "Been drinking, Teresa?" From the counselor, she got Ritalin, and from the classroom teacher she heard, "Honey, I'll pray for you." In Teresa's words, *"She thought that would fix everything. She never even thought . . . that this kid really needs some help."* Sharon, not being disruptive, successfully eluded any notice from school people: *"I can remember going through the day starving to death. No breakfast and no lunch and getting home and still no food. That went on for years."* When she was 16, she slipped away from school altogether. Both Sharon and Teresa were aware that they were only attending school because it was the law. No matter what the reason, both of these children knew that they were being sent to school to keep their parents and the school out of trouble and not because of anyone's interest in their individual needs.

Amidst all this chemical dependency and other addictions, sexual child abuse, general neglect and chaos, and physical and emotional abuse, however, three families tenaciously enforced rules about schoolwork.

Although the chaos that Violet described in her three-generation home could not have contributed to an atmosphere of study, Violet described her mother as *"being big in the schools"* and making homework and school attendance important values. Violet continued to attend school and complete her homework despite the abuse by the boyfriend and even later when living with a father who would not have insisted. But even though Violet's mother insisted on homework and diplomas, she refused to acknowledge or attend her daughter's early graduation.

Sylvia's family also had rules about homework and school attendance. Although Sylvia's father's rules about homework, grades, and school attendance were occasionally enforced by his beatings, her stepmother was the one who routinely checked her homework and helped her with the things she did not understand. Her father made the rules and punished if they were broken, but he did nothing to check or help her with any schoolwork. Her stepmother did nothing to stop the sexual abuse happening to Sylvia, but she was tenacious about supporting Sylvia's education. Sylvia not only was a National Honor Society student when she graduated from high school but soon after completed an associate's degree in college. Although inappropriately enforced by threats and beatings, this is the first family on the continuum to have two parents show standards and involvement of any kind about school and education.

Denise's family's emphasis on education could be seen every evening when her mother continually helped her struggling brother with his schoolwork. When Denise needed any help with her homework, it was usually received from her father. There were lots of teacher–parent conferences in this family, although not usually about Denise. Finishing homework was a must for both children and was enforced by both parents. This is the only family on the continuum to have both parents involved to the point of helping with homework.

The fact that the education levels attained by these five women matched so closely with their families' schoolwork standards, their families' participation in their education process, and the degree of safety each girl experienced in the school setting poses several questions. For a child abused at home, time spent at school may be perceived as the only time of safety in their lives. If the school setting, however, becomes perceived as unsafe and abusive like home or associated with other abuse in their lives, then it is only logical that such children would become less willing or unable to participate. The "degree" of perceived safety at school appeared to be closely related to the educational "degrees" attained at school by these five women.

It could not be determined, however, from the data in this study what, if any, connection existed between this safety factor and tenacity as a factor. Tenaciously enforcing standards about education and participating in that process appeared to make a significant difference in level of education attained even within incredibly abusive and dysfunctional home settings. For Violet, the goal of graduating from high school was so instilled while she was living with her mother that she attended school while living with her father even though she felt he would not make her go if she did not want to. Violet even finished her homework at her abuser's apartment after being raped by him on a daily basis. For Sylvia, homework had to be checked before being allowed outside to play. And Sylvia had to achieve A grades to avoid beatings. For Denise, homework had to be done before the family togetherness of watching television was allowed. It is also likely she vicariously benefited from observing the major parental efforts made to help her brother with his schoolwork.

These five families demonstrated the entire range of levels of parental interest, support, and tenacity toward their children's education. From nearly zero levels by any parent or stepparent through varying levels by one or more parents or stepparents to high levels from both biological parents. It is possible that within such inconsistent and unsafe home environments, consistent rules about school and homework actually could be perceived by neglected and abused children as the only consistent interest shown by anyone toward them over the years. At least in that one area of their lives, at least one parent appeared to really care about what happened to them. And because very little else in their lives was "normal" or anything they could really talk about with anyone, rules about homework and grades and school could have felt normalizing. Maybe you could not talk about your dad's beatings, but you could talk about his insistence that you get A grades. What is most surprising is the fact that these varying levels of parental interest, support, and tenacity toward school could have made such a remarkable difference in continuing aspirations about schooling despite the continuation of some incredibly chaotic and dysfunctional environments throughout the childhoods and into the adult lives of these women.

One thing none of these participants mentioned was experiencing anyone outside the family showing an ongoing interest about their schooling. At least three of these girls had at least one extended family member who showed extra caring to them outside of their nuclear family situation. Although portrayed as being very caring to them in general, none of these folks were portrayed as showing any specific interest in their schooling. Teresa's principal was the only school personnel identified as making an effort on behalf of any of these children. Unfortunately, it was not an effort that Teresa was able to receive. No other information about this interaction with the principal was found in the data, so persistence on the part of the principal is not known. None of the participants perceived any school personnel as someone they could talk to about any of their problems.

Although the sample size is small, there were two possibilities that did not show in this data. Although both women who did not graduate high school later obtained their GEDs, none of these women as children saw education as a way to escape their abusive backgrounds. There was no example of a family who devalued education producing a child who achieved educationally. Even the achievers excelled despite their circumstances and not because they saw it as a way to better themselves or to prevent abusive circumstances as adults. The other configuration that did not show up in this data was the family who tenaciously valued education producing a rebel who would have little or nothing to do with it.

The data from this study begs the question of caring as a factor of tenacity and points more towards two other possibilities. Tenacity alone may be a sufficient factor to make a difference in educational achievement. Or the consistency of tenacity over time may be experienced as caring even when provided in an uncaring manner or environment, especially to abused and/or neglected children. For children from such unstable environments, tenaciously holding to rules about school and education may feel stabilizing. If either is the case, both parents in abusive dysfunctional homes and schools, social workers, foster parents, and other resources external to the home environment may have more of an opportunity to contribute to the educational success of such children than previously considered possible.

6

You Are Students AND Parents: Messages from and Modeling by a Day Care Teacher in an Urban High School

M. Lynne Smith
University of Cincinnati

This ethnographic study focused on a group of low socioeconomic status high school student parents and their children who attended a child-care center housed in the parents' high school. Smith focused her findings on the phenomenon of learning to do school, which, as the data stories here reveal, the toddlers certainly did learn. But what was also happening, was a relationship of trust and care between the parents and the center's lead teacher. The teacher was tenacious in insisting that these adolescents define themselves as students, and just as vigilant regarding their development as loving parents to their preschool children. This chapter begins to soften the paradox of institutional neutrality. Although the institution wears blinders to real life outside its purview, the staff, teachers, and administrators may not.
—Editors

* * *

I been knowin 'bout school all my life, 'cause, 'course, I was a student my own self. But when my son was in the day care, I learned 'bout bein a parent and talkin' to a teacher 'bout my child. The day-care teacher, Miz Hurter, she send

home reports and she talk to me 'bout what he good at and what she workin' on with him, and his little art works, and we had lunch meetins where she talk to the mothers 'bout what the children learnin' and she send home the words of those little songs they sang. So, when he start singin' on the bus, I knew the words too and I'd sing. Then, when he start kindergarten, the teacher did the same things as Miz Hurter. She send his work home with him for me to see . . . and progress reports. Some of my friends afraid to talk to their children teachers. Not me. I'm good at it. And my son know if he do wrong, the teacher gonna tell me, and if he do good, she gonna tell me that too.
        —the 20-year-old mother of a first grader

This chapter describes some aspects of a day-care program that, I contend, accomplished far more than its stated purpose. Ostensibly, the program's purpose was caring for infants and toddlers so that their low-income, high school-age parents could finish school, knowing their children were being cared for in a safe place. However, the kinds of teaching and learning that took place in that day-care setting went beyond the scheduled, structured, deliberate teaching of art, music, and storytime. The day-care program, as implemented by the lead teacher, dealt with affective and cognitive aspects of toddlers' development and the development of their high school student parents, both as parents with skills in communicating with teachers, and as educational consumers claiming a voice in their children's learning.

   Much of what the preschoolers and their parents learned came from the physical setting of the program and the social interaction of teachers–aides–toddlers–parents. But the most important single factor in preparing toddlers for primary school and preparing young people to be parent educators was the day-care program's lead teacher. Her mentoring and modeling, her tenacious efforts to teach the "structures and processes" of schooling, and her insistence that young parents take pride in their responsibility for their own and their children's learning, together, served as a bridge between home culture and school culture. They helped children learn to function as students and their young parents to be both students and parents of students. Au and Kawakami (1991), recognizing the schools' widespread failure to meet the needs of minority students, discussed the need for educators to "attend explicitly to minority students' ownership of what is learned" (p. 280). Au and Mason (1983) urged educators to work together to develop a "hybrid" culture in classrooms, and Au and Kawakami advocated a shared understanding of the possible rewards of schooling. Swadener and Lubeck (1995), in offering the metaphor of *"at promise"* to counter the prevailing construct of "at risk," urged both educators and parents to think in terms of "collaboration and power-sharing rather than patronizing assistance, respect rather than pity, and belief in potential rather than failure" (p. x). In this day-care program, high school students were repeatedly and consistently urged to take ownership of their own and their children's learning and development, working with the day-care staff to maximize their children's and their own learning. The day-care lead teacher exemplified what Swadener and Lubeck advocated; her view of preschoolers and their young parents as learners and her insistence that the young parents take responsibility not only for their own education but for that of their childrens, were the heart of the day-care program and are the heart of this chapter.

By their participation in this day-care program, both the toddlers who attended and their high school student parents learned how to "do school," how to operate within the culture of urban U.S. public schools, attending regularly, interacting with teachers, having activities at home that supported school learning, and feeling some control of, some power within, their own school lives. Polakow (1993) reminded us that day care for the children of struggling families has an impact on only a small percentage of the large number of children economically eligible and in need of day care, and that "innovative, or sometimes merely pleasant and well-run, subsidized programs that make the world a little better for poor families on the edge, that ease the stresses in poor mothers' lives have always had to fight for their continued existence" (p. 101).

This program lost the fight for its continuation, a fight for funding and support that the day-care lead teacher fiercely waged. No longer are students at this urban high school able to have their children in a day-care setting within their school. Although the city newspapers shout the news of annually increasing drop-out rates and increasing teen pregnancy numbers, no studies have been done to show how many students are giving up on the city schools because of a lack of support services such as affordable day care. Thus, the day-care lead teacher has returned to a home economics classroom and the day-care facility has been remodeled for other uses. The children she worked with in day care have gone on to elementary schools, and it is their classroom successes and their parents' interactions with their children's teachers that are the true trophies of the day-care program's success. Polakow (1993) reminded us that, "Neither the teacher nor the school can cure the ravages of poverty; but a classroom can become a buffer world, firm ground on which to stand, a place to belong, to feel empowered to question, to experiment with entitlement" (pp. 160-161).

For the 11 children I observed in their kindergarten through third-grade primary school classrooms, a large portion of their preschool lives was spent in the day-care center. Some were there 8 hours per day, 5 days a week, from 7 weeks to 4 years of age. This day-care center was, by design, a "buffer world" not only for them but, just as importantly, for their young parents, a place to belong in the world of school, a place where the high school students began to learn how parents and teachers interact, a place where their children began to learn what a school is, what a teacher is, and what it means to be a student.

Specifically, what did the toddlers learn in the day-care center? What did their parents learn there about day care, about school, and about the complex, layered relationship between home and school? Can what was learned in that day-care situation be observed in the children's classrooms now and in the relationships their parents have with teachers? Who envisioned what could be learned and how that learning could be encouraged? How was the relationship between day care and student parents established and maintained? What does this tell us about tenacity? The answers to those questions are, in essence, what this chapter is about.

DESCRIPTION OF THE LARGER STUDY

This chapter focuses on one view of a part of the data collected for a larger, longitudinal ethnographic study. The focal population for this larger study was a group of 14 low socioeconomic status (SES) female and male high school students, most African American, and their children (ages 7 weeks to 4 years when the study began), several of whom were enrolled in a day-care center housed within the large, urban high school their student parents attended in a midwestern U. S. city. The initial 2-1/2-year ethnographic study focused on reading and writing in the school and home lives of the student parents and in the day-care and home lives of their preschool children (Smith, 1990, 1991).

Since that time, the focus of the study has been data collection and analysis largely focused on the elementary school lives of 11 of the children, who are now enrolled in Grades 2 through 5 in the same midwestern U. S. city, and the parents' interactions with teachers and other school personnel in the elementary schools their children attend (Smith, 1993). Data collection for the larger study has now taken place for 8 years. For the initial 2-1/2 years, data were collected in three kinds of sites: (a) the day-care program housed within the vocational building of the high school attended by the student parents, (b) the high school (classrooms, lunchrooms, offices, auditoriums, and extracurricular activities of the student parents), and (c) the homes of the student parents and their children.

From 1990 to 1997, data were collected in the classrooms of 11 elementary students (the children of eight student parents) who were toddlers in the day-care program and in their homes. Participant observation in all these sites has involved data collection in several forms: written field notes, structured observations, time sampling of activities, photographs, formal and informal interviews, audio taping of activities, a collection of artifacts, and a journal maintained throughout the research.

For the study reported herein the initial 3 years of field notes, structured observations, interview transcripts, and audiotape transcripts were reread and recoded, with a focus on the day-care lead teacher's activities and interactions. The subsequent data set was reread and recoded, looking for connections/references made to the day-care program and the day-care lead teacher by the children and their parents, and connections/references made to the ideology of the lead teacher. For coding, ideas from hooks (1994) vis-à-vis learning, learning communities, and teachers as role models, and ideas from Polakow on cycles of failure, erosion of play, and denial of autonomy to at-risk children were employed as lenses for revisiting the data. The patterns discovered during this process reveal the impact of the lead teacher's tenacious relationships with the student parents, on their own completion of high school and movement into other kinds of postsecondary schooling, and on their children's subsequent school lives.

The eight young people who were high school student parents during the first portion of this longitudinal study graduated from high school (six of the eight) or passed the GED test (two) during or shortly after the first part of this research and, during the second portion (1990 to 1997) were working at full-time jobs (three) or were working part-time jobs while attending community colleges (two), a state university (one), a technical school (one), or a city-funded job training program (one). The majority (six) were still single parents; two have married and three have had additional children since leaving high school. Seven of the eight are African American; seven of the eight are female.

In interviews with family members, I asked questions of and about three and four generations of the families of these 11 children. In all the families, this was the first generation to attend some kind of organized educational program prior to kindergarten or Grade 1. Perhaps not coincidentally, this is also the first generation in which no child has had to repeat kindergarten or Grade 1. In six families, the young parents are receiving no public assistance money or housing. In five families, the student parent was the first family member to graduate from high school, and some have gone on to further education or training. All the young parents describe themselves as very concerned about and very involved in their children's elementary school education. Significantly, their children's teachers echo and confirm their interest and active involvement in their children's education. "Learning to do school" in the day-care program, seems to have paid off, in a variety of ways, for both the children and their parents.

NARRATIVE FINDINGS

In the pages that follow, the physical space and daily activities or routines of the day-care center are described and compared to the physical space and daily schedule/activities of the primary classrooms in which the same children have attended kindergarten and Grade 1. Then, social interaction is described in both the day-care and primary classroom settings and adult–child interactions in the day-care setting and in the primary classroom settings are compared. In all of these areas, the influence of the day-care lead teacher, Becky Hurter, in establishing a foundation for school, and making that foundation explicit for the young student parents, is very important, for both the children and their parents. Day care could have been simply a babysitting situation. Direct instructional activities could have been ignored. Art and music activities could have been far less varied; instead, Mrs. Hurter opted to structure the space, the schedule, the activities, and the social interaction in ways that would prepare both the toddlers and their parents for the years that would follow day care.

Physical Space & Daily Scheduled Activities

The physical setting of the toddler's portion of the day-care space, arranged by Mrs. Hurter, prepared the toddlers for the primary classrooms they would enter after leaving day care; by design, it could have been a kindergarten room. The toddlers' indoor space was a large, carpeted, rectangular room with a long wall of large windows and another long wall of one-way glass for observation of the room by staff, student parents, or other visitors. One end of the room contained cubbies for the children, with their names above their individual cubbies; near the cubbies were a wooden jungle gym and slide and a piano. There was an area with large blocks, toys, tables and chairs, another for a play house area with child-size kitchen appliances and furniture. Another section of the space contained a record player, a selection of children's records, and a book rack. There was an open area used for story and song circles, a large bulletin board, a dress-up box of clothing and wigs, and an entrance to a bathroom with child-size fixtures. There was an art area with small easels, an eating area with a tile floor, tables, chairs, highchairs, and sinks; a diaper changing area; and a stack of cots for use at nap time. The outdoor space for the toddlers was paved and fenced, with wagons, tricycles, balls, and other toys. It was not used daily, but in the spring and fall, on days when it was not raining and was not too hot or too cold, it provided a change of environment for the toddlers, within a safe space.

When I interviewed each of the 11 children I followed for the entire longitudinal study, during the first months of their kindergarten year, I asked each to tell me about their kindergarten room. Our interviews took place in their homes, before I visited their kindergarten class, so, with each of the 11 children, I was asking a 5-year-old to describe for me a classroom I had never seen. All 11 mentioned in their descriptions the cubbies, *"lockers"* or *"hanger wall"* where they put their belongings; the record player, tape player and/or television set; the dress-up or make-believe area; the art area or materials; and books. Ten of the 11 mentioned the toilet(s) and tables and chairs. Eight of the 11 mentioned the area of the room where they eat lunch or have a snack (the others have lunch in a cafeteria). Seven also mentioned shelves holding books, paper, toys, puzzles, and/or art supplies. When I asked during the interviews if they had ever been in a room like their kindergarten room before, all 11 mentioned the day care space. They referred to it as *"my old school,"* *"my before school,"* *"my school whened I was little,"* or *"my school that was Mama's school, too."*

I think that the daily schedule of the day-care program also helped prepare the toddlers for kindergarten and their subsequent school years. A normal, daily schedule in day care began with free play, morning songs and greetings, then bathroom time, breakfast, free play and individual and small-group art activities, organized group activities (including story reading and song circles), bathroom, lunch, nap, bathroom, snack, and more free play. Mrs. Hurter made deliberate efforts to have each child involved in what seemed to be free and unstructured play that was actually carefully planned for multiple opportunities to exercise small motor skills (puzzles, dressing and undressing dolls, etc.) and large motor skills (walking up and down stairs, climbing on a wooden jungle gym and slide; building with large wooden blocks; hopping, moving head, arms, and legs in response to song instructions, etc.). Toddlers' finished artwork, with the child's first name in a corner, was hung in the windows or on a wall to dry. Every two or three days, art work was taken down and given to the children to put in their cubbies, to be taken home and shared with family. Lyrics of the songs sung regularly (e.g., "Good Morning," "Have a Seat," and "The Eensy Weensy Spider") were put on paper and distributed in cubbies, to be taken home. Parents received oral and written reminders from Mrs. Hurter that these songs were known by their children and would be fun to sing at home.

Participant observation in the kindergarten classes showed many similarities to the physical setting and the daily schedule of activities of the day-care center. The 11 children had seven different kindergarten teachers, in five different schools, over a period of 3 years. All of their kindergarten teachers reported in interviews and informal conversations that they knew the children had been in a day-care program and that, even before asking the parents, they often knew which day-care program because of the knowledge of the physical space, the materials available, and the daily schedule that the children brought with them into kindergarten. One teacher, who had one of the children in this study during the 1991–1992 school year and another during the 1992–1993 school year remarked:

> The minute Keisha[1] came through the door, she was ready to rearrange the room. She was sure that the piano was in the wrong spot and that there wasn't enough space to play house! I didn't have to read any records to know she'd been in a room very much like this one. She had no first day anxieties, no crying and missing mommy; she—well, she acted like she'd been here for years and I was the new person! This year, I thought of Keisha the first day of school, when Nathan arrived. He fussed about no yellow wigs in the dress-up clothes and no *driving car* in the toys. He didn't like sitting in chairs for songs; he urged all of us to sit in a circle on the floor. Both Keisha and Nathan were used to art in the morning, before lunch, and told me so each afternoon I had an art project!

Another kindergarten teacher, in the same elementary school, a teacher with 23 years experience teaching in primary grades, had two of the children I was observing in her classroom during the 1990-1991 year. She described both of them as:

> very comfortable with our schedule, among the few children who didn't fight the schedule at first. When we would sit in a circle during the first week, or sit down at tables to have our snack, some children would get up and start to

---

[1]This and the names of the other children and their parents are pseudonyms.

walk away. LaTanya or Dominique would grab them and tell them to sit down! I remember, I remember the first day of school, when a bell rang, some children began to cry, and LaTanya and Dominique comforted them. Dominique said: *"That's not nothin' . . . that's just a school bell. Don't cry."*

Social Interaction

School rules and procedures often differ from home rules and procedures. Because of the careful and consistent way Mrs. Hurter conducted the daily routine for the day-care toddlers, they started school knowing about nap time, about teacher's emphasis on the importance of sharing, and about following rules different from the rules at home. At ages 2, 3, and 4, the toddlers in the day-care program developed the ability to deal with rules, procedures, and persons that were different from their home experiences. For instance, toddlers who came into the day-care program at age 2 or 3 often initially resisted sitting down with the group for breakfast, lunch, or snack time. It wasn't until I observed them at home that I really understood their resistance. At home, most of the children were used to roaming around the table and/or around the room or from room to room during meal time, stopping intermittently to eat off the plates of any of the members of their extended families. Occasionally, they would sit on someone's lap and eat a few bites of food, but most of the time, they were in motion during meals. Thus, a teacher's insistence that they sit down at the table for meals and use silverware, was, at first, inexplicable. Gradually, they all adjusted, recognizing that one set of behavior was expected at home and another at day-care. hooks (1994), in discussing her work with college students from poor and working-class backgrounds, said:

> They express frustration, anger, and sadness, about the tensions and stress they experience trying to conform to acceptable white, middle-class behaviors in university settings while retaining the ability to "deal" at home. Sharing strategies for coping from my own experience, I encourage students to reject the notion that they must choose between experiences. They must believe they can inhabit comfortably two different worlds, but they must make each space one of comfort. (pp. 182-183)

This is exactly what the toddlers did—they learned to be comfortable in two different worlds; they learned and followed the rules of each, and the rules of day care were designed by Mrs. Hurter to prepare them to be successful with the rules of school.

Toddlers received positive, verbal feedback from Mrs. Hurter and the two teacher assistants throughout the day, praising them for following the day-care rules (i.e., picking up and putting away toys they played with, at the end of morning play time; using words like "please" and "thank you" and "excuse me" in their interactions with one another and with adults, sitting on the floor for some activities and in chairs for others). Examples of procedures the toddlers were expected to follow and feedback they received are a regular part of my field notes, as the following examples illustrate. The first example is from free play time in the morning, while the second is from lunch time.

2/26/88 Sierra (14 months) was walking toward the dress-up box, carrying the Fisher Price plastic record player, when Erika (26 months) walked by her and took the record player. Sierra sat down on the floor and sobbed. Mrs. Hurter, who had seen what happened, intercepted Erika, walked her back to Sierra and said to Erika: "Why is Sierra crying?" Erika shrugged. "I think you know, Erika. Tell me." Erika said softly, "*I tooked this from her.*" Mrs. Hurter: "What should you do now, Erika?" Erika gave the record player back to Sierra and said, "I sorry." Sierra smiled, got up, and walked away. Mrs. Hurter hugged Erika and said, "I'm proud of you; Sierra is just a baby, and we all need to be kind to the babies and not take their toys."

4/28/88 Miss Pat is feeding Missie in her high chair. She sits right in front of Missie and carries on a running conversation about the morning activities, the food for lunch today, the new child in the other high chair, the temperature (very cool today). Mrs. Hurter circled the toddlers' table as they ate, keeping them from leaving their chairs, urging one to eat, picking up a spoon and feeding one a few bites. Then she served the milk and gave applesauce to each toddler as they finished their pizza and slaw. Sheree gave a loud belch and Mrs. Hurter said: "What do we say?" Sheree grinned and said: "*Scuze me!*" Mrs. Hurter said: "That sounds so nice. I like it so much when you are polite and show your good manners."

There were times during the kindergarten and first-grade observations when something one of the children said sent me back to field notes from the day-care center. Learning "school rules" about food and about manners are common learning moments in my field notes in both day care and kindergarten/first-grade classrooms. On one occasion, a kindergarten teacher, in September, 1991 commented that:

I knew Shariah had been in a school setting before. She's the only child this year who wasn't upset about school lunches! I knew she'd had them before. When other kids pointed to food and said "What dat?" or What dis?" it was Shariah who explained. Of course, she was also very ready to be vocal about which foods she disliked, especially the taco salad.

This interview sent me back to field notes from 2 years earlier, when Shariah, as a 3-year-old, led a toddlers' lunchtime insurrection over the school lunch taco salad they had just been served. My field notes read:

The toddlers' parents are eligible for the Federal Free Lunch program, so their children qualify too. Breakfast and the afternoon snack for the toddlers are prepared here in the day-care program's kitchen, but lunch comes from the high school cafeteria, upstairs, and is exactly the same food the student parents have for lunch. Today, lunch features a large taco salad, served in a rectangular corn meal shell. Shariah took one look at it and said *"Look like doggie doo doo."* *"Doggie doo doo!"* Duncan repeated as Shariah turned the taco salad over, spilling food onto the table. *"Doggie doo doo! Doggie doo doo!"* several children started saying, laughing. The adults began to move around the table, quietly talking to individual children about "things we don't say at the table" and I had to walk away, so the toddlers wouldn't see me laughing.

Mrs. Hurter engaged the toddlers in dialogue throughout their daily schedules, not just at mealtime and not just to reprimand or teach manners. From the time the children arrived in the morning, she talked with them one-on-one, asking how their trip to school was, commenting on and asking them questions about their play: "Oh, I see you're building something with those big blocks. What is that you're building?" "Your macaroni necklace is beautiful; are you going to wear it today?" "I love your pumpkin picture; mommy will love it too, won't she!" Diaper changing and potty time were always occasions for conversation, and time spent reading aloud to toddlers was sprinkled with conversational exchanges about the book or about things the toddlers said about the book or the illustrations. Mrs. Hurter often carved out additional time for the toddlers (3-year-olds) to spend individually, working with her on letters, numbers, and colors, while the younger toddlers were napping. She set up tables, chairs, and materials for the 3-year-olds to use in the observation area on the other side of the one way glass, where the younger ones wouldn't be grabbing paper or crayons.

In this field note vignette, Mrs. Hurter is sitting at an Apple computer with a female 3- (almost 4-) year-old in her lap. They are using a Minnesota Educational Computer Consortium (MECC) Introduction to Math Concepts piece of software for primary children, designed to teach counting with the numbers 1 through 9. Nothing in the day-care program rules/course of study required the use of computers, but Mrs. Hurter felt strongly that the children would encounter computers in their primary classrooms and would have classmates who have computers at home; thus, she found ways to introduce computer activities to the 3-year-olds. It is nap time and the overhead lights are off; the glow of the computer screen is the only light in the room:

> I'm watching from over the teacher's shoulder; Sheree is on her lap and they are both looking at the screen intently. On the screen, across the bottom, are numbers:
>
> 1 2 3 4 5 6 7 8 9
>
> On the rest of the screen, a group of things appear, sometimes kites, at other times hats, people, houses, or cats. Each time a set of objects appears, Mrs.

Hurter and Sheree count them by touching each one with their index fingers and counting out loud. Then they touch the numbers on the bottom on the screen and count out the same number, then they count out the same number on the keyboard number keys, left to right across the keyboard. Then, they press the key of the correct number (the number of objects on the screen), and the number they pressed appears on the right half of the screen—and a smiley face appears on the left half of the screen. Each time this happens, Sheree laughs and claps and sometimes screams. Mrs. Hurter says: "Sheree gets to use the computer when she does something important every day. Sheree, tell Miss Smith what you do every day, so you can use the computer." Sheree: "*I take my nap.*" They return to the game, both intent on the screen. Mrs. Hurter gradually stops pointing and counting, and Sheree is doing each of the steps on her own.

The toddlers reached a level of comfort in the day care center, despite the ways it differed from their home environments—in physical space, in social interaction, and in rules—and, when they started kindergarten, it seemed clear to them that it was the day-care rules and not the home rules that usually applied in this new setting. Children who had not been in day care took much longer to adjust, for example, to school meal time rules, in the opinions of the kindergarten teachers. As one remarked:

Keith came to kindergarten ready to learn. He didn't "fight the system" is the was I'd put it. Being away from family, the routine here, the equipment and materials, the other children, getting his food tray and staying at the table until he finished eating, emptying his tray into the trash container . . . nothing bothered him. He seemed to have experienced a routine very much like ours; he knew the parts he played in that routine, and he taught other children those parts!

Parent-Teacher Interactions

It isn't just the children who had a high level of comfort in kindergarten and first grade. In my observations and interviews, the parents of the kindergartners and first graders, who were high school students in the earlier portion of this research, also had a high level of comfort in dealing with their children's teachers, some of it attributable to their experience with their children's day-care program, and the kinds of interactions they had with the lead teacher about their children. In describing an interaction with their child's primary-grade teacher, a student parent often refers to an earlier, similar interaction with their child's day-care teacher, Mrs. Hurter. One student parent, then 19 and the mother of a first grader, reported in October 1993:

In day care, they gave my child books for Christmas and I read her those books. At school, sometimes I went in the day care and watch Miss Anna and Miz Hurter read to the children. Miz Hurter, she told me that I'm my child's first teacher and her most important teacher. I thought about that. I got some more books at the library and I read to my daughter at home. I still do, mostly at nights. Her first-grade teacher say she can tell we read at home. She say DeNita likes to read 'cause I read to her and she want to be like me!

A first-grade teacher, describing parent-teacher conference evenings, in a January 1994 interview, said:

When we have conference times, I'm sorry to say this but we don't expect many parents, for lotsa reasons. Most of my children live in one-parent families. Some parents had bad school experiences themselves; they're intimidated by teachers. They expect to hear only bad things, and who want to hear bad stuff about their baby? I have to say that LaTanya's mother is here at every event. She goes to college, and she works, too—but she helped with a school field trip when LaTanya was in kindergarten, and now that she's a first grader, her mother is here for open house, for parent–teacher conference days. And, she doesn't wait for special events. When she drops LaTanya off mornings, at least once a week she comes in with her and asks me how things are going and talks about things they are reading and doing at home. I wish I had 21 other parents just like her. She does her job, takes pride in her child, and expects me to do my job. I feel like we have the same goal—helping LaTanya learn—and LaTanya knows it.

Three years before, when LaTanya was in the day-care program, her mother got in the habit of talking to the teacher, Mrs. Hurter, at some length, at least once a week. The following excerpt from a set of Friday afternoon field notes shows one of these interactions, laying the groundwork for the kind of parent–teacher conversation LaTanya's mother expected later:

When LaTanya's mother arrived after school to pick up her daughter, Mrs. Hurter asked her if she had time to talk. She nodded and Mrs. Hurter led her to a table away from the bustle of the cubbies, people going in and out of the room, etc. Mrs. Hurter began the conversation with: "LaTanya has really had a good week. She is more and more interested in storytime and she is learning her numbers, saying them and writing them. She's also doing more playing with other children instead of just playing by herself. Do you notice that at home too? (Mrs. Hurter then listens to LaTanya's mother's description of how there is a new family in the apt. next door, with a daughter LaTanya's age—the first time she's had another child her age in the apartment building to play with.) Mrs. Hurter ends their talk with praise for LaTanya's mom—her regular attendance, her reading to LaTanya and working with counting and letters. Mrs. Hurter tells her that she's a good teacher and that LaTanya is learning a lot from her.

The day care program provided an opportunity for the toddlers and their parents to learn about school: about the roles of teachers, students, and parents; about the daily schedule, physical environment, and daily routines; about the health/hygiene procedures of elementary school, like washing hands before meals and after going to the bathroom; about the things teachers value in students—like promptness, listening, cooperation, and sharing; and about the things teachers value in parents—like reading to their children, praising and displaying their artwork and other educational products, and communicating with their children's teachers. Repeatedly, in observations of their children, in lunchtime meetings, in one-on-one conversations with student parents, Mrs. Hurter reinforced the parents' knowledge of their children's routines, activities, and behaviors and encouraged their participation in repeating and extending the activities of the day-care center at home.

The Lead Teacher

What were the things Mrs. Hurter said and did that significantly contributed to the toddlers' and their parents' successful experiences with elementary schools and teachers after the toddlers' day-care experiences? What ideology seems to lie behind the organization and day-to-day activities of the day-care program and the interactions with the high school student parents?

Once a month, Mrs. Hurter organized a special two-period lunchtime event with the parents of the infants and toddlers. They ate lunch in the day-care center and then had a speaker, a demonstration, or a discussion of a particular topic, issue, or situation. In these sessions, the student parents learned the songs their children sang regularly, were given copies of the words to the songs, and were encouraged to sing the songs at home with their children. One speaker's topic was children's literature and reading aloud to children. Another speaker talked about first aid at home and the kinds of accident and poison prevention techniques the student parents should employ. In formal and informal interviews, Mrs. Hurter fretted about these special sessions, feeling that they were not frequent enough for covering all the topics that should be covered to help these young people become good parents. Her primary interactions with the student parents did not occur at these meetings, however; my field notes show that significant one-on-one teaching-learning interactions took place daily.

The kinds of daily, verbal interactions Mrs. Hurter had with the high school students as they dropped off their children in the morning and picked them up in the afternoon, after their own school day had ended, exemplified hooks' (1994) suggestion that "To engage in dialogue is one of the simplest

ways we can begin as teachers, scholars, and critical thinkers to cross boundaries, the barriers that may or may not be erected by race, gender, class, professional standing, and a host of other differences" (p. 130).

Mrs. Hurter attempted to engage the high school student parents in dialogue on a daily basis, talking with them about their children's attendance,
health, food intake, medications, activities, achievements, and interactions. The
following example of Mrs. Hurter's interactions with a parent on a Friday afternoon took place the day before Halloween in 1987.

> A female high school student came in the door, greeted her son, Marcus
> (*"Hi, baby, you have a good day?"*) and sat down on a chair with a heavy
> sigh. She turned to Miss Anna, one of the teaching assistants, and said
> *"Girl, I'm tired."* She looked at her son, then looked at Mrs. Hurter and said
> *"Different pants. Did he have a accident?"* Mrs. Hurter replies: "Yes, this
> morning, but several of the children did. We had them out trick or treating
> from room to room and it was a long time for them. He did not have any
> accidents this afternoon, and this morning was very unusual—they were
> away from the bathroom for too long a time." The mother nodded. Marcus
> got his rolled artwork and his jacket from his cubby; she helped him get his
> arms in the sleeves. Mrs. Hurter unrolled the artwork and showed it to his
> mother, saying: "He made the most beautiful jack-o-lantern. Won't it be a
> great Halloween decoration at home? Marcus beamed as Mrs. Hurter
> hugged him. He then turned to his mother; she hugged him too, saying
> *"This a wonderful pumpkin, Marcus. You a great artist."*

In this instance, as in many, many others, Mrs. Hurter interacted with a young
parent by being positive, sharing "good" things with the parent and even putting
a problem the child had (wetting his pants) in a context of the day's events and
the other children, so the parent did not feel responsible for or blame the child
for the accident. Mrs. Hurter also models praise for the child's artwork and even
a suggestion that putting it up at home would be a good idea. She also models
hugging the toddler, and the young parent then hugs him, too.

This next verbal interaction with a parent took place on January 21,
1988, again as a high school student parent was picking up her child at the end
of a school day:

> Erin's mother arrived and bypassed the staffmembers, going directly to her
> son's cubby to get his coat and mittens. Mrs. Hurter saw her and walked over
> to the cubby, holding Erin's hand. She spoke first as Erin's mother turned:
> "Hello. How was school for you? Erin had a great day!" The mother said
> quietly: *"Not so good. I had two tests today and I had to work late last night
> and didn't review like I wanted to."* "It's hard to work, be a momma, and be
> a student too," Mrs. Hurter responded. "But you are setting a very good
> example for your son with your work and your studying, and he is smart like
> you. He wants to know the names of things. He's a talker, like you. He

points to new toys or to pieces of equipment and says *"What's that?"* all day long. I can tell you're good about answering his questions and helping him learn new words. You're really helping him learn, and it will pay off later— he'll be a good reader, like you." Erin's mother smiled, took Erin's hand and said—*"I know what you mean; he asks me questions all the time too—you think that's good?"* "Oh, yes, it's very good!" Mrs. Hurter responded, "He can learn so much from you—you're his most important teacher!"

In this case, the parent seems to be avoiding interaction with the day-care staff, and Mrs. Hurter approaches her, not in a confrontational way, but greeting her and asking about her day, than listening, realizing that the young woman has had a discouraging day, and telling her something positive about herself and about her son, while also articulating and giving her credit for some of her son's attributes, things that are helping him be a learner. Directly, Mrs. Hurter conveys the message that a parent is a teacher—the most important teacher.

At times, Mrs. Hurter had to initiate conversations with the young parents that were potentially embarrassing, as in the next two examples from field notes. These examples also illustrate Mrs. Hurter's concern for the student parents as people, people in the full contexts of their daily lives, not just as students and not just as young parents. In each case, I was told about the specifics of the conversations by Mrs. Hurter and by the student parent later, because the talks were conducted privately, as Mrs. Hurter attempted to minimize the potential for hurt feelings.

3/24/88 *Observer Comment*: Mrs. Hurter took me aside today to tell me that there were roaches in Lakita's (Damion's mother) diaper bag this morning. Mrs. Hurter said she took the bag outside and sprayed it, then talked to Lakita privately about it. Lakita said there are many roaches in her apartment building and they can't get rid of them. She said that she and her brothers live upstairs above a man whose apartment is filthy and that even when they clean and spray their apartment, the roaches come back fast. Mrs. Hurter is concerned. She expressed to me her frustration, saying "Lakita is trying to be a good mother. She tries to keep herself and her baby clean, but it's not easy. She's taking care of herself and her son and her brothers. She can barely afford where she's living now, so it's hard to see moving as the answer."

And later that same month, on a Monday morning, Mrs. Hurter greeted an infant's father as he dropped off his son. The father, a high school student like the infant's mother, Meskie, had kept their baby for the weekend, because Meskie had to have some tests at the hospital and didn't have anyone else to watch the baby. Mrs. Hurter took the baby into the nursery, took off his outer clothing and, feeling a soggy diaper, carried him to the changing table, where she discovered that he was wearing not only the same clothing, but also the same decorated disposable diaper, she had put on him the previous Friday afternoon. Sharing the story with me later that week, she said:

The clothing was wet and dirty; the diaper was filthy; the baby's bottom
was inflamed. It made me cry and it made me angry. I cleaned him up and
put fresh clothing on him. Then, I thought about what I should say to
Meskie. I knew she was tired and sick, just out of the hospital. I looked up
her schedule and waited until later in the day, when she was in study hall,
to call her down for a talk in my office. I told her about the condition of the
baby, the clothing and the diaper, and she started to cry. Meskie told me she
had been worried all weekend, not trusting the baby's father to care for him
properly. He claimed he had diapers and everything he needed and that his
mother would be helping with the baby. I assured her that if she had an
emergency in the future, that she should call me to see if I could keep the
baby. I told her it couldn't be an every day kind of thing, but in an emergency she should call me.

Mrs. Hurter had copies of the student parents' school schedules; she sometimes
used their study hall period as a time to call them in for conversations about
and/or observations of their child through the one-way glass. The conversations
she had one-on-one at these times were designed to be instructive, setting examples for everything from reading a story aloud to treating diaper rash, to dealing
with biting or hitting. Watching through the one-way glass, Mrs. Hurter made
positive comments about the student parent's daughter or son, and then led the
way into an instructive commentary, as in the following example:

> Mrs. Hurter: Venus really enjoys story time. She is a good listener; you
> must read to her at home. (Parent nods, watching her daughter through the
> one-way glass.) Venus has gotten to the age where she can participate in the
> story. See how Miss Anna is stopping to ask questions about the story and
> the pictures? (Parent nods; Mrs. Hurter and the student parent watch for a
> few minutes.) See how eager Venus is to contribute—she wants to talk.
> Look how happy she is when Miss Anna praises her! (They continue
> watching together.) If you'd like to take some of our books home this
> weekend, you could read them to her. (Parent looks at books with Mrs.
> Hurter and picks out three she wants to take home.)

Not all the interactions took place with the young parents in person; they also communicated with Mrs. Hurter at other times, through notes or phone calls, initiating
the communication themselves, as this next incident from field notes illustrates:

> One of the almost-2-year-olds has pneumonia. Her mother has called Mrs.
> Hurter from the hospital four times today—and it's only 1 p.m. Mrs. Hurter
> said: "By the second call, I realized that she was at the hospital alone, she was
> frightened, and she was calling because she needed someone to talk to, so I
> talked to her for a long time and told her to call back whenever she wanted to.
> She has called me back twice more to tell me about Donata's x-rays and about
> what the doctors are saying. They may keep Donata at the hospital tonight. If
> she's still at the hospital this afternoon, I'll stop by there on my way home.

Rather than strictly defining her work hours or her work responsibilities as those in her written job description, this day was an example of the way Mrs. Hurter dealt with the full lives of the children and their student parents, looking not just at their absences but at the reasons for those absences, not just at the school day, but at the many complexities of the young people's lives, as high school students, as parents, as members of families, as part-time, minimum wage workers in jobs that left them little time to sleep or to socialize with high school peers.

The ideology behind the day-to-day interactions and activities of the day-care center was clearest to me in the interviews, both formal and informal, that I conducted with Mrs. Hurter over a 2-year period. It was in the interviews that she shared the things that were hardest for her, such as the difficulty she had separating her personal beliefs from her job. The following is from an interview conducted with Mrs. Hurter in the infants' room of the day-care center, in February 1988.

> One of the ninth graders has two children here in day care. I worry about her. I worry about her physically—she's just 14 and she had children at 12 and 13. And, I worry about her financially. The fathers of her children don't pay any support. I argue with myself about what I can and should say, and what I shouldn't say. My values are different from many of the parents. I don't want to say or act like my values are right and theirs are not. Theirs are theirs. At the same time, I worry that they don't have anyone to say some things that should be said. I was alone with this ninth grader yesterday, and I wanted to say "You have a nice little family; you have two beautiful children. Please think about not having more children for a while, so you can finish school and take care of these sweet babies you already have." I didn't say it. Maybe I will say it, but it's a struggle with myself, when things should be said, when I am overstepping my job. . . .

Similarly, when the mother of one of the toddlers was excited about her boyfriend being released from prison, Mrs. Hurter reflected, in May 1988, on what she wanted to say to this young woman:

> Latisha's boyfriend is getting out of prison. I know he used to hit her and I know he's a drug user. She has told me all that herself. I want to say to her, "Slow down. Don't be in a hurry to marry him. You're about to graduate from high school. Your goals, your life, what you want for yourself and your son may be very different from what he wants. You have changed since he went to prison. You may feel differently about him. And, he may feel differently about you." Will I say it? Probably not. Is that my job? These are young people's lives—and their babies' lives. It's very hard to draw lines about what is my job and what isn't.

The decisions Mrs. Hurter had to make about when to step into the student parents' lives and when not to were rarely easy decisions. No manual for high school home economics teachers (her area of certification) covered the kind of decisions she had to make on a daily basis. The day-care center operated by strict rules, rules made by the school and school system administrators, by the local board of health, by the guidelines of the Federal Free and Reduced Price Lunch Program, and rules from other sources. In an informal interview with Mrs. Hurter, she answered my question about what happened to the toddlers when their mother (or, in two cases, their father) missed school. Her answer gives some insight into how she viewed both the program's purposes and her own role within the program; I see her view here and in other situations as very consistent—*people are more important than rules*, and *context matters*.

> The rules say the children cannot be in the day-care program if the mothers are not in school, but the mother can be in school and choose not to bring the child in that day—if the child is sick or has a clinic appointment or something like that, and the mother has some kind of back-up or assistance from her own parent or someone else—the mother will sometimes be in school and leave the child at home. But if the mother is not in school, the rules say I'm not to accept the child. Now, I do make exceptions. For instance, one of the girls is in the food services program here in the vocational building and she cut the tip of her finger off in class this week. She has been at the hospital and at the clinic this week and her boyfriend brought her son in to me today. I'm not supposed to accept him when his mother isn't in school, but I did today, because I thought the circumstances were special. His mother is hurt, his normal routine is very disrupted, and he's been looking forward to our party today. I just decided to take him today, on my own responsibility. I explained to her boyfriend that I was taking the little boy on my own responsibility, and it was against the rules. Her son had only been with us a little over a week, and yet she was the only mother to send in treats for the party—I didn't want to disappoint her, and I didn't want him to miss the party.

The structure of social interaction in the day-care program, by Mrs. Hurter's design, helped prepare the children for social interaction in their kindergarten and first-grade classrooms. The daily routine, the rules, the activities, were all constructed with preparation for Head Start and/or kindergarten and the primary grades in mind. The children entered other kinds of schooling knowing that some times of the day were set aside for play and other times of the day were for more structured activities. Things forbidden in the day-care room—hitting, kicking, biting, or in any other way physically hurting someone else—were, of course, also forbidden in their next school settings. The disciplinary action called "time out," utilized by Mrs. Hurter and taught to the program assistants and to the parents, was also used in most of the educational settings the children encountered after day care. One kindergarten teacher commented, in October 1991 that "I knew Kevin already knew about time out before I explained it, because on the first day of school, he asked where the green chair was where time out people would sit. I told him we didn't have a green chair, we had a red one, but we still had time out. He accepted that." Kevin knew the important rules—he had learned them in day care. There are consequences for actions that teachers don't like; you have a pretty good idea of what those consequences are going to be; and, you can live with those consequences.

CONCLUSION

Kevin and the other children who experienced months or years in Mrs. Hurter's day-care setting learned a great deal about the expectations of teachers and the culture of schools. Kevin's mother, and the other student parents learned important lessons about parenting, about learning, and about how teachers and parents interact; in effect, they too learned about the culture of schooling. Mrs. Hurter was tenacious in her pursuit of ways to help young people continue their own education and invest, intellectually and emotionally, in the education of their children. Her vision for the student parents and their children was not an expectation of cyclical poverty and powerlessness; rather, it was a vision of possibility and promise that encouraged young parents to be the educational ombudspersons for their children. Caring tenaciously, Mrs. Hurter created situations and opportunities and made decisions that reflected her core beliefs about teaching and learning—people are more important than rules, so rules have to accommodate the needs of people; children are important people with needs that adults must pay attention to; and context matters—the contexts of home and of school, and the contexts of relationships that can be forged between homes and schools, in the best interests of children.

7

Holding On: Establishing Webs of Care and Connection

Debbie Zorn
University of Cincinnati

Stories of two drop-out intervention teachers illustrate their tenacity in establishing and maintaining networks of connection and care that include the students themselves, their families, other school personnel, employers, probation officers, and others. These comparative stories reveal that in some circumstances teachers can manage to refuse to give up on a student. Again, the difference between institutional policy and actual relationships between teachers and students is evident in these data stories.

Certain touch points exist between this conception of tenacious caring and Noddings' (1988) ethic of caring as moral education involving modeling, dialogue, practice and confirmation. The ability of the two teachers described in this chapter (Ms. Franklin's and Mr. Williams'[1]) to engage in dialogue with students allowed them to develop trusting relationships with their students, relationships that could certainly be seen as modeling care. These teachers also made realistic appraisals of their students in terms of their expectations, allowing them to confirm the students in ways that showed true understanding of their abilities and aspirations. However, whereas Noddings would attempt to inculcate a moral and caring ethic in children, this study suggests the possibility of a more tenuous, more basic first step—the provision of a culture and structure of schooling, a safe environment, where teachers might be allowed to develop tenaciously caring relationships with their students, where students might be listened to, appreciated for who they are, and encouraged to be who they might dare to become, and where they just might find a viable alternative to dropping out.
—Editors

* * *

---

[1]These and all other names used in this chapter are pseudonyms.

"You should have your homework in front of you, Dewayne. You know I'm displeased with you." It is 7:40 am. in Ms. Franklin's sixth-grade class. Six students sit with <u>Basic English Composition</u> books open on their desks. Ms. Franklin collects homework and gives a new assignment on writing topic sentences. *"I called your house last night, Dewayne, to see if you had your homework done, but the line was busy."*

Dewayne, a small 14-year-old wearing a blue and orange striped tee shirt and blue sweat pants, sitting in the middle of the classroom, shoots a paper wad into the basket by the door, looks around the room for approval and asks, *"Miss Franklin, how 'bout givin me a piece of paper?"*

"Dewayne, you know I'm going to continue to fuss until you get it together." A tall, muscular 14-year-old in a blue Teen Institute tee shirt and striped jeans strolls into the room and takes a seat in the back. Ms Franklin applauds, then asks Dewayne to come to her desk where he sits beside her and she begins to work quietly with him. Two girls in front finish their work and look at each other. Ms. Franklin tells them to review the spelling words on the board and, if they are comfortable with those, to look at their reading book. *"Dewayne, do you want me to call your mother to come and get you?"*

"She won't come."

Lifting the phone on her desk, Ms. Franklin replies, *"You know you've got to go if you can't get your act together."* Dewayne's face is wrinkled. Ms. Franklin puts down the phone and asks Dewayne to read from the English book and identify the topic sentence. Dewayne sits, his eyes flashing

"I'm not Mattel and I'm not Fisher Price. You do not play with me. Now, I should have the attitude because you don't do your work." She sends Dewayne back to his desk and dials the telephone. Dewayne puts his head down on the desk. Getting no response from home, Ms. Franklin gives Dewayne a piece of paper, saying, *"When you get paid, you're going to pay me for the paper."* She tells Dewayne she is going to take him home on her break. *"I'll take you to the door, open the door and put you in the house."*

"Uh uh. I'll put you out."

Another tall young man in a jade tee shirt and jean shorts, sitting in the front of the room, approaches Ms. Franklin's desk and shows her his work. Returning his book to the bookshelf, he moonwalks back to his desk and winks at me sitting behind Dewayne. Dewayne whispers to me, *"His name is Marcus."* I ask Dewayne what his name is. *"Bad boy."*

Ms. Franklin walks over to James, next to Dewayne, and checks his work. *"Beautiful, you got it!"* Hugging him, she exclaims, *"Your mama worked with you, didn't she?"*

Dewayne asks why she didn't check his work, and Ms. Franklin looks at his first sentence. Dewayne tells her, *"I knew how to do it. I just given up on it."*

Ms Franklin replies, *"You didn't give up, you were just trying me. I may still take you home. "*Dewayne points to the young man in the back of the room who has his eyes closed. Ms. Franklin calls to him, *"Richard!"* and

Richard answers, "I was just meditating." His face is in the bandanna in his hands. "I'm thinking about the economic deficit."

Dewayne tries to get Ms. Franklin's attention. He tells her he is going to rip up his paper and he rips off the bottom fourth, showing it to her. Ms. Franklin says, "It doesn't matter. I'm going to take you home."

In the meantime, Marcus is up from his desk and moonwalking around the room. Ms. Franklin drags his desk into the hall. Marcus takes his books and follows her.

Dewayne asks, "Why you do that?"

"Same reason I'm taking you home, because I care and want to do the right thing."

Dewayne and his classmates were 14-year-old students in a special intervention class for adolescents who had been held in the sixth grade and were more than 2 years overage. Their classroom was housed within a seventh- and eighth-grade middle school building, but was totally self-contained. Similar classrooms in three high school buildings were designed for 16- and 17-year-olds who had not been able to pass eighth grade. The large urban school district had recently instituted a "no social promotion" reform, and students at the third-, sixth-, and eighth-grade levels are required to pass special proficiency tests based on district promotion standards before advancing to the next grade. Once they are 2 years overage for their grade level, they are placed in these intervention classes. The intervention classes are considered to be a "last chance" for these youth, with the recognition that if they are not successful here, they are at significant risk of dropping out of school.

* * *

"Tardiness is becoming a problem."

"Some of you have job interviews today. Remember 'yes, sir and no, sir.' The first question is not, 'what's my day off?'"

"Applying formulas is one of the main things they're looking for on tests."

"Gotta do your homework."

"Do not get discouraged. Set goals and make them realistic."

These pep talks were the fabric of Mr. Williams' daily banter with his 16- and 17-year-old eighth-grade students, the tapestry on which he wove his academic lessons. All of the intervention teachers agreed that sustaining motivation was very difficult for their students, that, "These kids hate school, hate to be here."

* * *

At 9:20 the sixth-grade students leave for their one mainstream class—art, music, health, or physical education, and Ms. Franklin and I drive Dewayne to the large public housing project where he lives with his mother. Ms Franklin takes Dewayne to the door, knocking loudly until the mother wakes up. She takes Dewayne inside and explains to the mother that Dewayne has not done his homework and was not willing to work that morning Dewayne's mother promises to keep him home and punish him. Ms. Franklin says she will call tonight with Dewayne's assignments.

Driving back to school, Ms. Franklin says she is not sure yet whether Dewayne's mother is "being straight" with her, so she will call the home later to check up. She thinks a lot about Dewayne. She hasn't quite figured him out, but knows she is missing something that will turn him on. She says she tries not to embarrass students unless she knows they can do the work. "I teach the old fashioned way." She gives homework 5 nights a week and she believes she has to use parents as part of the process. This is my first day observing in Ms. Franklin's classroom, and she admits to me that she was nervous when I arrived that morning and wanted to "act professional—but I usually just act like a mother."

The next week, when I see Dewayne, I ask him about his day at home. He tells me his mother made him clean the house and he's not going to let that happen again.

THE INTERVENTION PROGRAM

The observations just described were part of a 6-month descriptive study of the pilot year of an intervention program conceived as a remedial program to allow sixth- and eighth-grade students who are 2 or more years behind to accelerate their learning to catch up to their age-mates.

Guidelines for the intervention program gave the following program goals:

1. Assist students to gain the maturity, skills, and knowledge necessary to function in middle/high school.
2. Mainstream students into their regular academic classes as a result of planned remediation and assessment.

The intervention classes had one teacher who had the responsibility of remediating four academic areas—language arts, math, social studies, and science for 8 to 13 students. Assessment tests were given at the end of each semester, and if the students passed any of the subject tests, they were supposed to then be enrolled in seventh- or ninth-grade "trailer" courses (which would begin midyear) for those subjects. Students needed to pass three of their academic subjects to be promoted to the next grade level.

These students were mainstreamed with the regular students for their music, art, health, or physical education classes. Students spent a half day at school and were assigned to jobs in the community for the remainder of the school day. According to the program's supervisor, the career exploration program was "supposed to be a [part of the] remedial program. Jobs are for motivation."

The urban middle school and high schools that housed these intervention classes drew a large proportion of their student population from three of the largest public housing projects in the city. The only factor that could be said to characterize this diverse population of intervention program students as a group was a history of high absenteeism. Of all the students 63% were male, and 67% were African American.

Most of the teachers in the intervention program exhibited high levels of commitment to the very difficult job of teaching and caring for a population of students who were most at risk for dropping out of school. Two teachers, however, were extraordinary. Ms. Franklin was a small African-American teacher, certified in vocational and adult education and with 3 years of experience teaching adult basic education. She said her experience teaching adults was helpful to her in the intervention program because she had "*seen what the outcome is*" when students drop out of school. Mr. Williams, by appearances, was as unlike Ms. Franklin as he could be—a tall, white science teacher and ex-coach—but very similar to Ms. Franklin in the way he related to students. One of Mr. Williams' students in the eighth grade program said, "Just about any book Mr. Williams can get for us to prepare for the tests, he does." By contrast, Ms. Miller, a composite of the other intervention teachers, serves to illustrate behaviors that are more typical of day-to-day student–teacher interactions.

The guidelines for the intervention program declared that teachers would be "caring, organized and academically oriented . . . [and] skilled in using the promotion standards." But, what does it mean to say that a teacher will be "caring"? Myriad teacher behaviors were observed over the course of the study that could be characterized as caring interactions. Many of these were procedures that were built into the career exploration program, such as helping students find and maintain jobs, and maintaining frequent contact with students' employers and parents.

Day after day, I observed teachers like Ms. Miller expressing and demonstrating obvious caring attitudes toward their students—concern, affection. and commitment. However, Ms. Franklin and Mr. Williams were two teachers who were clearly different from their peers in that their behaviors showed a *tenacious* quality of caring.

CARING AS COMMITMENT

Teachers like Mr. Williams and Ms. Franklin were committed to trying to understand each of their students, what did and did not motivate them, what may be troubling them, what might possibly turn them on to learning and achievement. Ms. Franklin would have liked to have had her students for more time for remediation and insisted on limiting this group's work experience to 3 afternoons a week, rather than 5, to give her 2 full days in class for academics. She used the promotion standards to structure her instruction, and she developed a grid to keep track of individual students' progress on each objective. She planned her lessons carefully so that students could get started on an assignment but not spend too much time and get discouraged. Her classes were conducted with high energy, giving the impression that there was not a moment to spare in her quest for academic success for her students.

Eight students comprised this class, four males and four females. Ms. Franklin believed the students were fairly comfortable at the middle school, but she understood that they were most comfortable when they were in her classroom, barely tolerating the mainstreamed classes. Two of the girls were too shy to eat in the lunchroom, and Ms. Franklin stayed with them in the classroom during the lunch hour. She worried about how to facilitate their adjustment to the school, afraid they would have trouble fitting in when they were finally promoted from the intervention class.

She was a strong disciplinarian, using isolation of students and calls to parents to enforce her rules and work expectations, which included homework in, at least, language arts and math 5 nights a week. She said she believed she had to involve parents to do this job. After a student was absent for 2 days, she always called the home, and she regularly called in the evening to check with parents on whether students were doing homework assignments.

Despite her image as a disciplinarian, Ms. Franklin obviously enjoyed the students and could have fun with them. When one of the bashful girls was called on in class and would answer tentatively, Ms. Franklin would tease her with questions like, "Are you positive, Rachel? Can you make me a believer? Bet me a quarter." Although she admitted that she has had allergies since she was a child and did not enjoy the outdoors herself, she accompanied the majority of her students to their work assignments 3 afternoons a week at a city park where they worked with a park naturalist to perform such tasks as cutting honeysuckle and rebuilding trails. Ms. Franklin insisted that the last 15 minutes at the park be used for free time—running and climbing in the woods, and one day, when she and the students were crossing a large grassy field to return to the bus, she spontaneously organized a foot race and participated in it herself.

She said the students had not really thought much about promotion until they took and failed the tests at the end of the year. Ms. Franklin obtained agreements from each of them to attend summer school with her to continue working to meet the challenge of the promotion standards.

This tenacious interest, characterized by a steadfast attitude of not giving up on the student, was well over and above the commitment usually expected of school personnel. The pattern of this tenacious interest, as it was exemplified by teachers like Ms. Franklin and Mr. Williams, usually included the teacher maintaining high expectations, working to get to know the student well and to engender trust, and building these qualities into networks of contact, connection and care—networks that formed a potential web of safety for these at-risk children.

CARING AS EXPECTATIONS

All of the intervention teachers struggled with understanding and implementing the new promotion guidelines and the implications of the guidelines for detailed record keeping of students' demonstration of individual skills. And, they were all concerned that failing a student who was trying, would mean certain dropout.

Tests for promotion were given at the end of the first semester in math, English, social studies, and science, and there were many failures. For the few students who passed one or more of the tests, the promise of trailer courses at the appropriate grade level did not materialize. Morale was low for both students and teachers. The difference, however, between students adopting an attitude of giving up on earning promotion to the seventh or ninth grade and an attitude of tempered optimism that the goal was still accomplishable, was, in some measure, dictated by the behaviors of the teachers. If teachers tried to circumvent the promotion standards or simply went through the motions of using them, students recognized the low expectations held by their teachers. For example, one of Ms. Miller's students said, "*She don't teach until just before the test . . . [She] gave us that little easy stuff.*" Another said, "*My vocabulary and math skills have decreased this year. She thinks we're stupid because we're from a poor environment.*" The students in this class felt that their trust in their teacher had been violated when they did not receive the academic assistance they had been promised.

On the other hand, those teachers who held high expectations for their students, expectations that they could indeed learn and would either pass the tests or be promoted by the teacher-certifiable rubrics, were able, against heavy odds, to keep more of their students attending school that year—even summer school—and working to achieve their goals.

CARING AS ENGENDERING TRUST

Trust was an important ingredient in teachers' abilities to find ways of working with each of the students. Students sensed the support they were receiving, support for their efforts to come to school regularly and on time, to maintain a job, or to develop academic work habits and achieve success in the classroom and on the tests for promotion. For the teachers who were able to demonstrate that they were committed to helping their students meet the promotion standards, most of their students felt that support and reciprocated with trust.

Some students also knew they could trust their teacher to be on their side in a difficult situation. One day, Mr. Williams received a call from the office at the end of third bell asking him to hold a boy named Danny because the police were at the school and wanted to question him. Mr. Williams got the police on the phone, inquired as to whether there was a reason for questioning Danny, and learned that there was no charge against him. Danny was not held in the room, and Mr.

Williams explained to the police when they arrived that he had an obligation to develop trust with his students. Months later, when Danny was accused of receiving stolen property and assault, Mr. Williams attended his hearing, testifying that Danny had not been violent in school and had been doing well in his class.

CARING AS KNOWING

Ms. Franklin's students were also able to feel that they could begin to trust her. Ms. Franklin had spent much time getting to know her students and reflecting on what would work to motivate each individual student—a motherly approach for one, seriousness or silence and eye-to eye contact for another. She believed most of her students had fallen behind because of a spectrum of behavioral problems in their elementary classes and that it was her job to "deprogram" bad school habits. She said that, each evening, she concentrated on two students, their behaviors, and what she could do to change their behaviors. Dewayne, she thought, was her biggest challenge, but she was determined to find the secret to reaching him.

Marcus, the moonwalker, a medium height, 13-year-old African American loved to laugh, and Ms. Franklin characterized him as the class clown. Sometimes, Ms. Franklin had to isolate Marcus in the hall to get him to do his work as he was often up from his seat in the classroom, usually moonwalking. One morning I observed Marcus and Dewayne grinning at each other with bubble gum spread over their teeth and gums. Marcus appeared to want the other students' attention, and could usually count on getting Dewayne's by making faces or talking to him.

Ms. Franklin understood that Marcus needed a strict disciplinary approach, occasional isolation from his peers, and regular admonitions about his true ability. (When she told him the 3 years he had spent learning his multiplication tables was enough time to have earned him a master's degree, Marcus consequently passed his multiplication test.) Ms. Franklin learned much of this through discussions with the boy's mother, whom she talked to every other day for the first 3 weeks Marcus was in the class, gaining insights such as the fact that his mother thought he was lazy, but that she was willing to work on academics with him at home. Marcus was absent only 1 day.

Ms. Miller did not know Anthony, Michael, and Robert as well as Ms. Franklin knew Marcus. Anthony was a small 15-year-old African-American boy who, when he attended, was always at least 30 minutes late to school. His mother reported that she sent him out every morning, and his father sometimes called to see if he had made it to school. Anthony had difficulty reading, and his teacher estimated his reading to be on a first-grade level. Ms. Miller also reported that Anthony had difficulty interacting with other students. Anthony was already a participant in another intervention program—the criminal justice system, having spent 10 days during the school year at the juvenile detention center on a gun violation. Ms. Miller had numerous conversations with Anthony's probation officer, which she reported had little effect on Anthony's behavior. Ms. Miller told Anthony he had a "bad attitude" and had referred him to the vice principal for lying and making up stories earlier in the school year. Anthony often sat in class with his head on his arms or slumped over in his seat with his head on his hand, eyes closed.

Michael, a tall 16-year-old African American who wore his hair in a loosely interpreted version of dreadlocks, lived a distance from school, nearly halfway across the city. Halfway through the third quarter, Michael moved in with a brother to be closer to school, a move that had little impact on his sharply declining rate of attendance. Ms. Miller made many contacts with Michael's mother, whom she believed had little control over her son. Neither Michael nor Anthony was able to keep a job. Their teacher told me Michael refused to cut his hair to be able to work in a fast food restaurant, and she thought that Anthony was probably not capable of working because he had "a chip on his shoulder." Anthony and Michael were suspended for 3 days for fighting with each other. When Ms. Miller talked about these two boys, she expressed deep concern for them, and affectionately dismissed their difficulties in school by saying, "*Michael and Anthony are just immature.*"

Robert, a muscular African-American 16-year-old, like Anthony, had already found his way into the court system. He told me, "*I was in court from April through October for assault. I broke ___'s nose. Found me not guilty . . . . This year I be by myself most of the time. Ain't got no record yet.*" He said he went to three different private elementary schools until last year when he wanted to go to public school. "*I got in the wrong crowd. First couple of weeks I kept to myself. I do get a quick temper, though. Up here, everybody cool. Since I been up here [at the high school], it been goin' all right.*"

Robert had big dreams of playing football for the high school, something he was not permitted to do as long as he was in the intervention class. He played basketball, had won a boxing tournament for the housing project recreation center, and claimed to be the "secret weapon" on their gymnastics team. Robert's mother got him his job at the recreation center where he opened the center in the afternoon and supervised children younger than himself in the weight room and on the basketball court. Robert was the one student who was usually present in Ms. Miller's high school intervention class first thing in the morning. He had passed two of his promotion tests the first semester, but found there was no room for him in a mainstream first bell class. Robert said Ms. Miller's class was "*kinda bored*" because there was nothing to do but work crossword puzzles, watch movies, or read the newspaper or *Sports Illustrated*, so he sometimes came in late. Talking about academics, Robert told me, "*Concentration, that's the thing. Plus, I got a tutor. Lady [from a local industry] comes, works with me and my sister on her lunch hour.*" He said his tutor came to his house at least twice a week and was kind of like a family friend. When I asked him if his tutor helped him with his schoolwork, he said "*some,*" but he still hadn't finished the first packet of work Ms. Miller had given him. When I asked Ms. Miller about her contact and involvement with Robert's tutor, she said she did not know about her, despite the fact that she had maintained contact with Robert's mother and had Robert in a one-on-one classroom situation nearly every morning.

Ms. Miller structured many of her classroom lessons around the issues and concerns she perceived to be important to the teenagers in her class. One morning, as the students watched a videotape on dating and sex, Michael, noticing that all the actors were White, said, "*I couldn't learn nothing from them. They do things different.*" Michael proceeded to ignore the video, concentrating, instead, on constructing an elaborate tower with magic markers. Later, when I asked Ms. Miller, who apparently had not heard Michael's comment, if she thought Michael would have liked the film better if it had Black actors, Ms. Miller told me, again, "*Michael is just immature.*"

Mr. Williams' high school intervention classroom was different. Mr. Williams had worked hard to develop ways to engage the students in his class with examples and illustrations for his academic lessons that would touch their interests and concerns. Mr. Williams also decided that he could use my presence in his classroom as a check on his perceptions about his students, and he regularly discussed his students with me, in depth, sometimes calling me at home or at my office if something happened that he thought was significant or puzzling. Mr. Williams was very familiar with Randy's school, home, and work life and recommended that I follow Randy through his school day and visit the boy's job with him.

Randy was a soft-spoken, somewhat unkempt white 16-year-old who said he did not like academics, but said he had just recently begun to understand their value. He had previously attended a number of schools, where he claimed he was "just lazy, just didn't do the work." Although Randy did not agree that everything taught in school is important, he said he recognized that graduating from high school, and maybe even college, were essential to having a good job. He liked the no-nonsense approach of the intervention class' concentration on the essentials, but said he still did not see how all of it was useful, especially math. During a math lesson, as Mr. Williams proposed a problem about the height of a stack of drywall, Randy disgustedly corrected him, "*You wouldn't stack drywall that way, you would stack the sheets on their sides.*" Mr. William sometimes accused him of skipping steps in math, but Mr. Williams' use of practical, "real-life" examples about spending a paycheck or getting a car loan, usually seemed to engage him.

Riding the bus for 2 hours to get to school, Randy always arrived about 30 minutes late but well ahead of most of the students in his class. Randy had been arrested once riding a dirt bike, and he told the story of the police chase with relish. He also claimed to own a 1973 Chevy and to sometimes drive illegally. Randy's father worked in construction, and Randy had worked for him for about 5 years. He was proud that he had some practical skills so he did not have to "*flip burgers,*" and he wanted to some day own his own business like his father and his employer.

Randy worked in the afternoons at a lawnmower repair shop, owned and operated by a friend of his family. After school, he usually took a bus downtown, then transferred to another bus to get home, where he got on his bicycle and rode it to the shop, eating lunch at a local fast food restaurant. He had become acquainted with his employer when he took his family's lawnmower to be repaired the previous summer and showed interest in the business. The owner offered to teach him some things and give him a job.

Mr. Williams got much of his insight about Randy's abilities and interests from talking to Randy's supervisor. Although Mr. Williams was not always successful in making contact with Randy's parents, he frequently visited the lawnmower shop and kept in steady contact with its owner. Unlike Michael and Robert's teacher, Mr. Williams and Ms. Franklin knew their students, inside and out.

THE WEB: CONTACT AND CONNECTION

When I took Randy to work one warm spring day, the small shop was filled with lawnmowers and was crowded with three customers. Randy and one other employee worked with the owner, and Randy hurried to help wait on one of the customers. Later that day he would go on the truck to make service calls. Randy told me the training for his job had taken a long time, that he was not very fast, but that he had now worked up to doing five to six lawnmowers a day. Randy's supervisor told me he was "a good kid, doing a good job, although he tends to get flustered when things get busy." His supervisor said he talked to Randy earlier in the year when he thought Randy was getting mixed up with the wrong crowd, and Randy listened to him. The supervisor told me he knew Randy's parents and grandparents and "you can understand a kid when you know where they come from."

Randy was lucky. He not only worked with a caring employer who knew where he came from, but this caring adult was part of a network that included family and school. Mr. Williams kept close tabs on Randy, not only for his academic progress, but also his work and social adjustment and his personal maturation. Regular contact with Randy's employer and attempts to contact Randy's parents completed the web of care that was a result of a tenacious interest in this young man's success.

Care, contact, and connection were intended to be fundamental to the operation of this intervention program. However, they were not always pursued with the tenacity exemplified by Randy's network of caring adults. Thomas, a student in Ms. Miller's class, had a similar, but somewhat different experience in the intervention program. A 16-year-old African American, Thomas started the school year at the high school without having been promoted to the ninth grade. Once his status was discovered, he was sent back to the middle school. Thomas and his mother learned about the intervention program and asked to have him admitted. Ms. Miller reported that Thomas' mother had control in the home and used the threat of sending Thomas back to middle school to keep him attending and working in the intervention class. Thomas was known to have skipped school, but the instances were rare. His job placement was at a small fast food restaurant with about four tables where he worked at the drive through window, wearing a headset and taking and filling orders. Thomas liked his job, working from 3 to 11 p.m. and afterward walking home by himself to the nearby housing project. He gave his mother $25 a week from his earnings to help with bills. The teacher talked to Thomas' mother regularly to let her know how well he was doing in the job component of the program and how pleased his supervisor was with his work. The beginning of a web of care had been carefully woven for Thomas.

Thomas made a point several times to tell me when he would be working, and he smiled broadly at me when I visited the restaurant, seemingly proud of his position. He was equally proud of his work in the intervention class such as the posters on alcohol and drug use that he traced from overhead transparencies, and he liked helping other students in the class.

Homework, however, was no more a habit for Thomas than for any of the other students. Once Ms. Miller asked the students to recopy a composition for their writing portfolio at home. The next day when no one had done it, Ms. Miller was particularly disappointed in Thomas, saying, "I know you did it. You said you were going to." An opportunity to activate the web of care to support Thomas in carrying through with his commitment to complete his assignment, had been missed.

Also proud of his job was Richard, a 14-year-old African American in Ms. Franklin's class who worked in the university admissions office. Ms. Franklin called him a *"bright kid who likes to be first to finish,"* although his work often contained mistakes as a result of his haste. She thought he was behind in school because of personal problems. Richard had moved many times and now lived with a grandmother. Unlike Thomas, whose mother would have been likely to back up the teacher if she had been called, Richard's grandmother did not offer much support when Ms. Franklin called about the youth's homework. One morning after one such call, Richard said, *"She was tore up, wasn't she? Come home with a big bottle of T-bird."* Richard went on to explain that he had left his homework on his grandmother's dresser for her to check, but that *"this morning she was knocked out."* The teacher did not know if this was one of the fibs about his homework she had caught him in before, but this time said only, *"We're going to do this at lunch time."* Tenuous though this web of care was, it was an active and supple one, and strength was added where needed to make up for the weaker strands.

Ms. Miller, who was particularly successful in getting her students placed in jobs, also had significantly lower classroom attendance than any of the other teachers. When I asked her about her contact with parents about students' attendance, she said, shrugging, *"Parents have been called by teachers for the kids' entire school career.*" However, our study suggested that the combination of proactive teacher and interested parent or guardian working together with regular communication, often with the help of an interested third party such as a job supervisor, usually appeared to indicate higher student attendance rates and more solidly documented measures of success.

Ms. Franklin not only called homes, she put miles on her car if it meant an opportunity to affect the attendance or academic behavior changes she was trying for with her students. Rachel and Jill, the two shy girls in Ms. Franklin's class, were both 14-years-old, white, wore their hair in a ponytail on top with the back and sides cut very short, and were both inclined to truancy—together. Ms. Franklin had caught them once in the spring when both girls were absent and she called their homes on a "gut feeling" that something was amiss. Again, during summer school, both girls missed school on the same day, and after school Ms. Franklin drove to the university dormitory where they had afternoon jobs. The girls were not at work, so the teacher continued her search, driving to Jill's house, getting Jill's mother, and driving both of them to Rachel's house where they found the girls alone in the house. The girls' story was that they had taken the wrong bus to work, ended up north of the city, and had just returned. Not believing them, Ms. Franklin acted angry, elicited the assistance of both girls' parents to stay "on top of the girls' behavior," and obtained the agreement of the parents to personally bring the girls to school for the rest of the summer. This teacher used her carefully woven web of care to prevent two of her charges from slipping away from her tenacious hold.

WEBS OF CARE

Michael and Anthony's music teacher, an African-American male minister from an inner-city church who had been a volunteer teacher and who was trying to enlist other adults to volunteer in the schools as mentors and volunteer teachers, had a unique appraisal of the two boys viewed by Ms. Miller as being unreachable or dismissed as being immature. He believed that Michael was "*a good kid; but he is a follower*" and that "*What Anthony needs is nurturing.*" The music teacher had a simple prescription for success for these students: nurturing by adults who care. Data from this study supported his prescription, suggesting that, when at least one adult took a tenacious interest in a student, that student stood a better chance of staying in school and progressing.

Ms. Franklin and Mr. Williams are not model teachers in the sense of innovative instruction or curriculum. And, like the other intervention teachers, they had small classes—Ms. Franklin had a class of only 8 students, and Mr. Williams had a class of 13. They had telephones on their desks, a luxury in this urban school system; and they were responsible for classroom instruction for only half a day, giving them time to make the all-important phone calls and visits with parents and employers. Furthermore, the high school principal admitted that the students in this pilot intervention program were there because someone, likely a parent, had shown interest in having them in the program in the first place.

The Ms. Millers of our study, who shared the same advantages of class size, instructional responsibilities, and equipment, and who approached their teaching jobs just as responsibly and ethically, nevertheless carried out their jobs more in keeping with the culture of schooling as most of us know it. Ms. Miller, Mr. Williams, and Ms. Franklin all maintained the same professional behaviors of caring interactions. But, Mr. Williams and Ms. Franklin built tenacious relationships that contributed to a greater level of success with their students.

Although they, like the other teachers, did not necessarily "relate" to their students' backgrounds and interests, they made it their business to try to understand where the students were coming from, to get to know them as individuals, accept them for who they were, and attempt to build trust. They consistently communicated and held the students up to high expectations, and they used whatever networks existed or could be built to support these students, enlisting the help of other significant adults in their lives.

Teachers like Ms. Franklin and Mr. Williams recognized that teachers cannot do it all, and so they took steps to facilitate regular contact and connection with parents, guardians, employers, probation officers, and any other adults who were important to the lives of their students. They also created and supported connections with other adults in the students' school lives, like the music teacher, to strengthen the web of care. Through persistence, continuity, and contact, they exemplified characteristics of what we call *tenacious caring*.

8

A School with a Mission to Care

Barbara Huston
University of Cincinnati

This final story describes a small urban alternative high school that served a population of students who had troubled and intermittent educational pasts. This is a school that struggles to abandon institutional neutrality. The staff as a whole—security guards, secretaries, teachers, administrators, counselors, and even visiting researcher—are committed to holding on to these students until they graduate. The data story reported here focuses on one recent graduate and her relationship with two staff members—the principal and the school secretary. These relationships illustrate tenacity as experienced up close in day-to-day encounters.
—Editors

* * *

"I never knew I was smart. I was just a smart aleck."

These were the words of Stephanie Weaver[1] valedictorian at Kent High School, as she reflected on her school history. Five years earlier she was enrolled at Lincoln, another high school in the same school district, where she regularly skipped school. In the fall of each of the next 3 years, she enrolled at Lincoln and by the spring of each year she dropped out. In the midst of those 3 years she even enrolled at Ferndale, a suburban high school, but even there the pattern did not change. She explains,"I went to Ferndale for a quarter, and I dropped out of there, too. I did go to some of the classes, and I was totally left out. There was nothing there for me."

---

[1]This and all other names of people and places in this chapter are pseudonyms.

From dropout to valedictorian is Stephanie's story. As a student who had found a myriad of ways to skip school and to drop out annually, Stephanie changed dramatically. She now had a new image of herself. She described this change: *"This school here has motivated me to do a lot of things. When I came here, I smoked and I didn't come to school that much. But when I came here, I quit smoking and I quit doing a lot of things. I just got my life together. It's changed my life a lot."*

This chapter describes a small urban high school serving a population of students who have had troubled and intermittent educational pasts. The staff as a whole—security guards, secretaries, teachers, administrators, counselors, and even visiting researchers—are committed to retaining these students until they graduate. The part of the study reported here focuses on one recent graduate and her relationship with the people at the school. These relationships illustrate staff persistence and tenacity experienced in day-to-day encounters.

The dropout rate in schools in the large city urban environment is a national problem of critical dimensions. Among inner-city youth nationally, the dropout rate approaches one in four. This problem has been addressed by school districts in a variety of ways, including use of special classes, use of special schools, early intervention in elementary and middle schools, mentoring, and encouraging parental involvement. Although each of these methods has met with some success, the solution to the problem remains elusive.

To better understand the dropout problem and to discover factors that contribute to at risk students' successful completion of high school, a series of case studies were conducted at Kent High School in Watertown. Watertown, like other large urban school districts, experiences a significant dropout rate among its youth and has addressed this problem in a variety of ways with limited success. The year of this study, for every 100 students who entered the ninth grade in Watertown, 60 could be expected to graduate. One of the ways Watertown dealt with its dropout rate was by establishing Kent High School.

Kent High School was established to serve students with deficient prior education, students at-risk of dropping out before graduation. Indeed, all the students at Kent had tenuous academic and attendance records before enrolling at Kent. Many had even dropped out of another high school, some more than once, and returned to attend high school at Kent when offered the opportunity.

Opened in the late 1980s, Kent was intended to be a nontraditional academic experience for former dropouts and students at risk of dropping out. Each student enrolled at Kent met one or more of the following criteria:

- Reading at or below the sixth-grade level.
- Truant more than 40 days per year.
- Of school age but not enrolled in school.
- Parent of one or more children.
- Expelled.

- Adjudicated by the justice system.
- Overage for their current grade.
- Unable to compete in a traditional high school setting.

Five years later, the year of this study, 182 of the 372 students (49%) enrolled at Kent remained there. Only a little more than 30% had dropped out of school and 21% had withdrawn for a variety of reasons. Furthermore, Kent students' scholastic achievements—core courses passed and promotion rates—and attendance were found to be comparable to those of students in the other district high schools. Their discipline rate was substantially lower than at other district high schools, and students' attitudes toward school were found to be more positive than those of high school students district wide. This record raises the following questions: Why were students who were unsuccessful at other high schools, having success at Kent? And, what factors at Kent fostered this change?

To investigate these factors, data were collected from various sources. Attendance and performance records were provided by the school district's central office. The principal and selected teachers were interviewed. Observations were conducted; and nine students were interviewed. Four of the students were selected by the director of the reading program. In turn, each of these students recommended another student. One student was curious about the interviews and asked to be interviewed. Some of the guiding questions and leading statements of the student interviews were:

- Who are the people at Kent?
- Tell me about a typical day at Kent.
- Tell me about a typical day for you at Kent.
- What is a typical day like in your life?
- How does your story differ from the other students' stories?

Interview data along with observation data were analyzed for common threads. Numerical data provided by the school's district office was analyzed statistically to obtain an academic and attendance profile of the Kent students. Through the analysis, several common themes related to factors contributing to successful outcomes for at-risk students at Kent were identified.

The remainder of this chapter is divided into two sections: In the first section, Stephanie's story is presented; and in the last section, common themes are presented and discussed.

"IF YOU CAN DREAM IT, YOU CAN ACHIEVE IT"

"*I love it here!*" Stephanie spurts as she begins her story. "*The faculty is really great!*" She smiles, then continues, "*They're always helping me, and everybody's eager to help.*"

Six years ago Stephanie was enrolled as a freshman across town at Lincoln High School. The school population was *"humongous."* Stephanie felt uncomfortable at Lincoln. She skipped classes regularly, indeed almost daily. She explained, *"When I did go, just walking through the halls made me feel,"* she paused, shuddered, and then softly began, *"I don't know. I didn't like it. The classrooms, the teachers were there, they'd give you work, you did it; and if you didn't, oh well."* She stopped and shrugged her shoulders and added, *"I don't know. It's hard to explain the feeling. You could sit in the back of the class and be nobody there. You were there but you weren't."* She attended math class only a few times; before the end of the year, she dropped out of Lincoln. The next 2 years were echoes of the first; she enrolled and she dropped out. She even tried another school and dropped out.

The size of the student body at Lincoln (more than 1,700) frightened Stephanie. *"Five? six hundred, I don't know. It's so huge. So many kids. There is about 30 kids in a classroom, maybe 20. And it's scary in a big school. If you got into a fight or if someone was picking on or messing with you, what's the chance of them [i.e., school officials] finding who it was even if you didn't know .. It was awful."*

Stephanie arrived at Lincoln *"real"* early. Without delay she walked to the park next to the school and met with her friends under the bridge. Here her school day began. She smoked several cigarettes; and then she began to walk. That year, she walked and walked. She walked around the block, she walked to the bakery, she walked to the gas station. Weather had little effect on this pattern. She walked in the heat, she walked in the rain, she walked in the cold. When it was zero or below, she walked to the gas station, she sat in the bathroom, warmed up, and then, walked some more.

Two years ago Stephanie enrolled at Kent, where her metamorphosis from *"smart aleck"* to *"smart"* was encouraged and nurtured. When she speaks of this developmental process she emphasizes the importance of her relationships with the people—students, administrators, faculty, counselors, staff, and volunteers—at Kent.

The small brick building that houses Kent High School rests on the edge of a major waterway. It is yellow (Or is it tan? It is hard to tell). The brick is dirty and dingy. The concrete walkway and stairs around the outside of the building are chipped and cracked. It is an older building, built in the early 1900s as an elementary school. It is surrounded by mature trees that attest to its age. Barges drift down the river in the background. Indeed, this quiet sylvan setting belies its urban location.

As I walked up the crumbling steps at the side of the building and entered the building, my initial impression was one of gloom. Although it was midday, the entrance was dark and dreary. Another researcher, who had come with me to introduce me to Kent's principal, commented on the gloomy entrance as we climbed the stairs. At the top of the stairs, just inside the doorway, was a security officer, sitting behind a table signing class admission slips for tardy students. Behind him a bright mural was painted on the wall. The background was yellow, and in large blue letters the maxim, "If you can dream it, you can achieve it." jumped out. When I first saw this maxim, I thought it was there for the benefit of the students. I soon learned that other individuals at Kent also dreamed.

After greeting us, the security officer inquired as to our identities and how he could help us. Pointing ahead, he directed us to go to the end of the hallway and turn left. The first door on the right would be the school office. Finding our way down the hall and around the corner to the office, we were greeted by Ms. Nickel and Ms. Anthony, two secretaries. As we waited for the principal, we engaged in small talk with the secretaries and each other. Several students also came into the office and talked with the secretaries.

Stephanie's entrance was followed by Ms. Nickel's eyes. A comely blond with a walk that was light and bouncy, she approached Ms. Nickel's desk. They exchanged a broad grin. Then Stephanie and Ms. Nickel chatted, and she bounced out. As this animated young woman left the office, Ms. Nickel leaned back in her chair, turned toward us, her face aglow, and announced proudly that Stephanie had won a tuition scholarship to attend a national leadership conference for outstanding high school students. Ms. Nickel added, "Stephanie is looking forward to going out of town for the first time in her life." She noted that Stephanie had always wanted to travel, especially to see the ocean.

During our short wait we observed several other students enter the office and converse with the secretaries. Then the principal—a tall, dark, expensively and fashionably dressed, striking individual—entered the office, greeted us with a smile and handshake, and invited us into a small adjoining office. We had begun to ask questions when we were joined by Ellen Howe, the director of the reading program. Together they described the school community and outlined the major features of the program at Kent.

Kent was a redirection high school that served Watertown's former dropouts and students at risk of dropping out. It was begun 4 years earlier with students in Grades 9 to 12 and served a small school population of less than 300 students. The student population was predominantly African American (90%) and female (60%).

Critical features of Kent included reduced class size, often under 15; a mentoring program; a tutoring program; support services including social services and psychological services; day-care service for the students' children; and a "connect" policy. (The teachers were urged to connect with individual students, and each student was urged to connect with a teacher. In many of these connect relationships the teacher would call an absent student, inquiring whether the student was in need of help.)

The principal explained that students came to Kent for a variety of reasons and through a variety of paths. Some were referred by their previous schools for truancy, pregnancy, or failure and being over age. Others were referred by other Kent students. Still others were self-referred. The admission process at Kent had three steps: (a) the prospective student must complete an application, (b) the student was interviewed along with a parent or guardian, and (c) the student must attend a 2-week orientation. After successful completion of this process, the student was admitted to Kent.

Stephanie was 18 years old when she was admitted to Kent. Kent was much closer to her home than any of the other high schools she attended. It was about 1.5 miles west of the house where she grew up, *"all my life—18 years in the same house."*

She lived with 10 other people—her parents, a brother, a sister, the sister's baby, a half-brother, two cousins, a foster child, and the foster child's baby—in this seven-room house. The mother and two nieces slept in one bedroom, the father and her brother and half-brother shared another, as did her sister and her baby, and the foster child and her baby. Stephanie had her own bedroom. She explained that the crowding had increased over the past couple years, beginning when her mother's sister died and her mother received custody of Stephanie's two cousins. The census of this crowded household then increased once again with the foster child, and again when two babies were born within 6 months of each other.

Several days after meeting Stephanie, I sat at the far end of the library waiting for her. As Stephanie approached the desk at the front of the room, Ms. Howe, the reading program director, looked up, smiled, and leaned forward. Stephanie bent over the desk, and they chatted briefly. Then Stephanie looked across the room and saw me. She crossed the room to the old oak table where I was sitting, greeting me with a spontaneous comment, *"I love the teachers! They're really great!"* Turning her head toward two women standing near the card catalogue, she noted the school librarians. *"They always go out of their way to help me find information. I love to read. They always give me good books that are interesting to read. If I've read everything, they give me something new."*

However, Stephanie did not love mathematics. She commented, *"It's tough. I've had a lot of help. My teacher is very helpful."* With the help and encouragement of Mr. Klop, the math teacher, she passed algebra. She added that she did very well in the class. Mr. Klop helped her individually during class and after school, and a volunteer tutored her for 3 weeks. She spoke of the teacher and volunteer with deference, and credited them with her successful completion of the mathematics course.

The respect was mutual, and Stephanie's teachers spoke enthusiastically of her. *"For a long time Stephanie was asleep. Now she has wakened,"* rang the words of Mr. Mann, Stephanie's history teacher, who eagerly lent her history books and novels. Mr. Mann recommended her and guided her through the process of vying for a national leadership scholarship. She received the scholarship, one of many honors awarded to her. For 2 years she received the city's top academic female award during the Appalachian Student Celebration. She won the District Watertown Academic Leadership Award, and she was chosen by her district's congressman as one of a few students to attend the recent presidential inauguration. She was also selected to serve on the Kent school planning committee, consisting of district officials, community representatives, and teachers and staff from Kent.

Kent cultivated close relationships between students, faculty, and other school personnel. Stephanie commented on her relationship with the principal: *"The principal, she's wonderful. She's just like one of us. She's fun to be with. She's pretty cool,"* a comment that was reflected many times by other Kent students.

Stephanie contrasted her experience with the security officers at Kent with her experience with the security officers at Lincoln. Every day, electric golf carts driven by security officers at Lincoln scoured the surrounding area for truant students. In defiance she ran and hid from them. As she compared the security officers at Kent with the security officers at Lincoln, she reported, *"We have security guards, but they're not like your normal security guards. They're real friendly. If you have a problem with somebody, they'll talk with you. They talk it out. They're not quick to take you to the principal and get you in trouble. They'll try to help you try to work things out."*

"Friends for life!" was Stephanie's description of her relationship with Emily Smith, her mentor. Emily, a young computer sales person, was matched with Stephanie by the director of the mentor program at Kent. Emily (as Stephanie refers to her) and Stephanie met regularly. Often they ate together at a local restaurant, where after a leisurly meal, they lingered and continued talking and chatting, bringing each other up to date on happenings since their last meeting. Their history of shared experiences were varied and numerous. Sometimes they shopped at the mall, went to the amusement park, or to the swimming pool, or took short trips to other places of local interest. Other times were quietly spent at Emily's home, perhaps coloring Easter eggs or making ice cream. It was not uncommon for Emily's sister, a college student, to join them.

Stephanie's family was also an integral part of her newfound success. To reward this success and to encourage her to stay in school, her father bought her a car. She noted, *"My dad bought it for me last year when I became responsible and started going to school."* She hesitated and continued slowly, *"I think he still doesn't trust me that much. He is afraid I might mess up again."* Suddenly her voice became clear and her words crisp, as she expressed her resolve to persevere, *"but I am not going to. No way!"* Stephanie's graduation from high school in June would be a notable achievement and a family milestone. She would be among the minority of Appalachian students graduating from Watertown high schools where 70% of the Appalachian students drop out before graduation. She would also be the first member of her family to graduate from high school.

As Stephanie considered her future, she dreamed about several ideas:

"I want to be an oceanographer, but I don't live next to the ocean, and I'm kind of afraid. I don't know what it's like. But I've always loved water. I've swam on swim teams, dive teams. I love to swim. . . . There is so many things I want to do with my life. I may want to go into x-ray, or doctor. I might be a doctor. If I go into politics, I'm convinced I might be the first woman president. Just a lot of motivation. I'm ready."

"IT TAKES A WHOLE VILLAGE TO RAISE A CHILD"

Kent High School is a part of a village, a small village, where people know each other and are known by each other. At Kent there is focused effort to ensure that each student has the opportunity to succeed. Each student's success is enabled by the caring people at Kent.

The year of this study, Kent owed its success, at least in part, to its small student population (200 to 300 students). The smallness of the student body spurred Kent's faculty and staff to cater to the individual needs of the student. Indeed, Stephanie found the ambience even more intimate than a village. "It's like a family, really." Smallness and intimacy were two qualities identified by the principal as essential for Appalachian students.

Although Kent's approach to retaining students and enabling them to succeed may not be a panacea, the commitment of the staff as a whole, to retaining these students until they graduated was found to be facilitated by their caring relationships with Kent students. A tenacious form of caring was found to be demonstrated by many caregivers at Kent—teachers, secretaries, security officers, administrators, counselors, janitors, district personnel, day-care workers, parent educators, community volunteers, students—in a variety of ways.

The staff at Kent was carefully selected from experienced individuals who exemplified a caring demeanor. Many of these hand-picked individuals had been co-workers with the principal at another high school. The caring role cascaded down from the school's administration, and receivers of care became givers.

The staff at Kent recognized that they were a part of the village and that student success is enhanced by support and connection with significant others outside the school. Hence, one of the admission requirements was a preadmission conference where the student must be accompanied by a parent, guardian, or another adult who supports the student's desire to enter the school.

This concern for support and connection with students' families was also demonstrated by the faculty and staff at the day-care center for the children of Kent students. The center, which had developed and implemented a comprehensive program providing developmentally appropriate activities for all children, was located about 5 miles from Kent near the downtown area. Although there was no transportation to and from the day-care center for the children, transportation was provided for the student parents between the day-care center and Kent. One hundred children—infants, toddlers, and preschoolers—were cared for during the academic year, with approximately 50 children attending the center on the average day.

The day-care center curriculum and faculty emphasized parental involvement. The faculty assisted the student parents in identifying and utilizing community resources. Students who had children attending the day-care center were required to enroll in a parenting class. In addition to the classroom lectures and presentations, faculty members watched for ways to engage student parents in discussion, to provide guidance, and to answer questions when the student parents were present in the classroom, especially before and after school.

Parenting education was integrated with the high school through activities such as the book club. Student parents were encouraged to join the book club, which sponsored holiday activities at the day-care center, giving student parents opportunities to engage in enrichment activities with their children.

The size of the high school—less than 300 students—fostered identification and early intervention for emerging problems. The small classes enabled teachers to customize learning experiences for the students. The teachers regularly worked with students who had been absent from school. The principal routinely reviewed the attendance and tardiness every morning. If students were absent or tardy they received a telephone call (if they had a telephone) from the principal and the "connect" teacher to determine if they had a problem and how the school could assist them in finding a solution. The students were carefully watched and cared for. It was also the principal's policy to telephone with a wake-up call students who were repeatedly tardy.

Several students who were interviewed commented on the connect policy. In the words of one student, *"The teachers are real concerned. If you miss days, they call you."* Another student commented, *"If you're not at school they call your home. They'll come to your house. They'll bug you to death. They're sweet. They really care. I know every one of my teachers care. The teachers that I don't have this year that I had last year, I always see them. They're always asking me how I'm doing. Congratulating me and stuff like that."*

Caring is of vital importance to the Kent students' success, a quality that Stephanie recognized and credited for her new found success. *"There are just a lot of caring people here."* Stephanie said in reference to Kent. Whereas at Lincoln, she reported, *"They just didn't care."* Indeed, Stephanie blamed the absence of caring for her previous failures and credits the caring atmosphere at Kent for her success. *"Everybody is real caring. They want you to come to school. They want you to be prepared, and to do your work."* This perspective was corroborated by other students. One student who previously attended three different high schools, told why another students should consider Kent. *"I would encourage them [other students] to come here because you get the help you need here. . . . This is the best school I've ever attended."*

Caring, as it was found to be exemplified by the staff at Kent, is a tenacious quality. It includes, but is not limited to, concern. It is a quality in the character of a giver that is experienced by a receiver. The giver is persistent. The receiver cannot easily cast off care from the giver. Like a burr that is difficult to pull off a sweater, caring is difficult to be cast off by the student. Caring is not limited by time or effort but is characterized by the steadfast commitment of the giver. It requires stamina and painstaking attention and persistent guidance. Indeed, caring cannot exist without a willingness to hang on and not release. This watchful attention requires commitment, steadfastness, and determination.

Stephanie's story is a story of a young woman who was "brought to life" by tenaciously caring people at Kent. Stephanie's recommendation, *"I think they should make more schools like this one here [Kent],"* speaks for itself.

9

Tenacious Caring: Where Do We Go From Here?

Bram Hamovitch
Cleveland State University

When all the stories were told, the narratives written, we decided we needed to challenge our own conclusion that tenacity brings to the concept of
caring a strength, almost a fierceness that is not immediately evident in the
word and its interpretation in the educational literature. It is too easy to
assume that caring is about affect; that teachers, especially elementary
school teachers, could make slight adjustments in their pedagogy to include
a bit more personal attention, some comforting touches, a larger supply of
tissues, and just a bit more concern. Although Noblit (1993a) had already
begun to deconstruct that notion of caring in his ethnographic study of a
very powerful second-grade teacher, it still seemed that the concept was
vulnerable to being interpreted as "merely sentimental, unreflective caring"
that can at least be "effective," if not "emancipatory" (Eaker-Rich,
VanGalen, & Timothy, 1996, p. 231).

Not wanting to be guilty of contributing to this soft and teacher-blaming
interpretation, we sought independent confirmation that the quality of
tenacity genuinely moved the conversation about U.S. children in urban
schools into a different, more accurate because more problematic, space.
We invited Bram Hamovitch, a critical theorist whose work had already
directed some lobs at the sentimental interpretation of caring, to read our
stories and critique our construct. In the pages that follow, he does just that.
—Editors

* * *

117

This chapter explores a number of questions that I raise in response to my reading of the other chapters included in this volume. By raising questions, I am attempting to start a dialogue that can help us better understand how the concept of *caring* (whether tenacious or not) can be included as part of a broader set of understandings of the problem of serving "at-risk" or marginalized students. This statement of purpose makes two assumptions. One is that this collection of chapters is in fact one that explores the central issue of at-risk students. This, I believe, is obvious from a perusal of the students being cared (or not cared) for, as depicted in the chapters. Second, I am assuming that a close-up look at caring needs to be supplemented by integrating this concept with others already used by other researchers to help us understand the experience of at-risk youth within schools. The isolation of one concept or phenomenon may be useful in its infancy, but is not likely to sustain much explanatory power in the long run.

For the majority of the researchers here, caring is unproblematic, needing little or no clarification. Zorn (chapter 7) however, borrows from Noddings (1992) in her definition of *caring* as "moral education involving modeling, dialogue, practice and confirmation." Zorn argues that teachers should be encouraged to develop caring relationships with their students, "where students might be [will be?] listened to, appreciated for who they are, and encouraged to be who they might dare to become." In another explicit attempt to define caring, Huston (chapter 8) declares that "it includes, but is not limited to, concern. It is a quality in the character of the giver that is experienced by a receiver. The giver is persistent. The receiver cannot easily cast off care from the giver. Like a burr that is difficult to pull off a sweater, caring is difficult to be cast off by the student." By using the word *persistent*, Huston moves us toward an understanding of the new concept of *tenacious caring*. There is an additional time element introduced here that is not explicit in the concept of caring. The tenacious care giver is perceived as being persistent, dogged, and determined in caring for the other. Both concepts are relational because they focus on the idea that caring manifests itself most importantly in the quality of relationships that people have with each other. Huston suggests (and others imply) that the care of the caregiver encourages the recipient to be grateful for the caring. This, in turn, makes the cared-for person more inclined to meet the caregiver's expectations.

My first reaction to the chapters here, however, is surprise at their apparently a-theoretical nature. It is important to point out that I am an educational sociologist, and that training within this field may account for a number of the comments I make in this chapter. I should also reveal that I situate my research within critical theory, a paradigm that explores questions about institutional arrangements that permit deviation from what one might loosely call a "just" society (Gibson, 1986). Although I know that the editors deliberately set out to collect "stories of urban school survival" where the researchers "let the data speak" without "theoretical constructs" (Pitman, chapter 1), I would argue that this information needs interpretation. As Kuhn (1962) pointed out, many researchers erroneously think their findings reflect truth or reality, and that science develops by the accumulation of individual discoveries and inventions. He argued that a particular set of findings is likely determined by such nonscientific factors as one's prior experience and by accidents of the investigation. By analogy, I suggest that the caring literature needs more explicitly stated paradigms within which to interpret its findings, which should be considered at various levels of abstraction (Mills, 1959). For the most part, the research in this volume limits itself to descriptions of microsituations, while containing only scattered hints of how these findings can be understood as being related to other factors. For example, Pitman (chapter 1) properly comments on the contradiction between business leaders helping urban students, at the same time that they discriminate against and exploit the students' parents and neighbors. However, her analysis ends there without further comment, leaving the reader to speculate about this contradictory relationship between caucasians and urban African Americans, and how it might influence relationships within schools that have formal links with White businesses.

My reaction emanates from the fact that there is inadequate discussion of the question of how to balance the apparent need to work within the existing system of schooling with a more critical understanding that certain groups of children experience barriers to success because of structural forces that lie within and outside schools. Demonstrating that some individuals are able to overcome barriers because of the tenacious caring of those around them is a level of analysis that intends to inspire hope. The implied solution is to provide all youngsters with a coterie of tenaciously caring adults. But how realistic is that solution in the broader economic and political context that we live in? It is important to keep in mind that this is only one among many factors that influence students' participation in schooling.

What follows, then, is a dialogue with myself in response to the chapters in this volume.

- *Is tenacious caring a new and more efficient way to manipulate children into doing what adults desire?*

In a sense, this is a loaded question, implying that adults do not always know what is best for students, and that they try to impose on them their own conceptions of appropriate behavior and culture. The collection of chapters in this volume appears to accept the notion that caring adults know what students need: high school graduation followed by college in the pursuit of a middle-class lifestyle. The researchers present an image of the caring adult working tenaciously by steering the young person in the "right" direction. For example, Huston (chapter 8) presents the story of Stephanie, the dropout who "changed dramatically" in response to the caring environment of Kent High School. Graduation from high school, any high school, is taken as an indication that caring has paid off. And perhaps it has paid off in the sense that many jobs in our society stipulate high school graduation as an entry requirement. However, when one looks more closely at this issue of Stephanie graduating from high school, a difficult question emerges: What does the completion of an alternative high school program generally achieve for its graduates (besides the credential that may or may not be identical to the one from a more traditional school)? The sociological literature indicates that there are significant differences in academic programs between schools (Anyon, 1981; Bowles & Gintis, 1976; Weis, 1985) and within schools (Oakes, 1985; Page, 1991; Rosenbaum, 1976). Van Galen (1996) found that even in a "caring" Catholic high school, the learning is largely passive and the students are stratified by gender and track. Teachers there speak of caring for their students, and yet have no conception of needing to empower them with a curriculum that allows them to successfully compete in the economy as adults. In short, there is evidence to complicate the simple model of tenacious caring paying off for disenfranchised students. It is possible to imagine that high school graduation reaps few economic or social rewards, depending upon the nature of the curriculum in the high school attended and the response of individual students to that curriculum.

- *Is tenacious caring a way to advance the ability of disenfranchised groups to compete in schools and in the economy?*

The descriptions in this volume suggest that the simple answer to this question is "yes." The vast majority of these chapters focus on individuals who lack valued resources such as income, wealth, prestige, and political power. They include settings such as a poor, urban school district (Pitman, chapter 1; Smith, chapter 6) an alternative high school for at-risk students (Huston, chapter 8), and a special intervention class for overage students (Zorn, chapter 7), and focus on individuals with characteristics such as low-income African Americans (Camblin & White, chapter 3), teenagers living on their own (Milgram & Briton, chapter 4), and students living in abusive households (Heydt, chapter 5). I caution the reader, however, from leaping to the unstated but implied conclusion that tenacious caring is the solution to weak school performance among disenfranchised groups. First, the data presented here were not specifically collected with the intent of supporting this conclusion, and contain only rudimentary evidence that suggests such a relationship. This is because many of the contributions are case studies of exceptional circumstances or extraordinary persons in normal situations. Second, ample research has demonstrated that other factors are involved in the alienation of students from school, such as curricular issues (e.g., Cornbleth, 1990; Cusick, 1973; Wehlage, Rutler, Smith, Lesko, & Fernandez, 1989); issues of race (e.g., Fordham, 1991; Ogbu, 1974, 1978; Solomon, 1989); social class (e.g., Anyon, 1981; Bernstein, 1977; Bourdieu, 1977); and gender (e.g., Brown & Gilligan, 1992; Woods, 1990); and issues related to school organization (e.g., Callahan, 1962; Coleman et al., 1966; Jencks et al., 1972). Thus, it can be stated fairly that caring (even of the tenacious kind) may be one element in the successful socialization of any child. But it should not be viewed as a panacea that will help to transfer resources to disenfranchised groups.

- *If one cares for another, whose values/culture will be used as the basis for that relationship?*

Do those who are on the receiving end of tenacious caring generally embrace or resist such efforts? These two questions are related in the sense that they ask about the quality of caring relationships that are sustained within schools. Elsewhere, I have described these as ones involving *institutional caring* (Hamovitch, 1995). This type of caring is defined as "concern by middle-class professionals for lower-class clients that takes place within an institutional context in which the caregiver 'looks out for the best interest' of the lower-class client" (p. 26). Unlike the studies in this volume, I found that many at-risk students resisted the caring overtures by the staff. This was linked to the fact that the caring by middle-class staffmembers brought them face-to-face with lower-class culture, which they attempted to neutralize and/or repress. Clearly, these and other similar analyses (e.g., Freire, 1970, 1973; Miller, 1991) have implications for the questions at hand. They suggest that middle-class caregivers have difficulties in shedding their ethnocentric tendencies (as, indeed, we all do). An attempt by middle-class caregivers to impose their values on lower class clients can create resistance. The result is a lopsided relationship in which the staff member yearns to care, while the clients/students put up with the relationship because the imbalance of power compels them to play along. What emerges, then, is an alternate image of caring within schools, one not quite so optimistic about the ability of caring relationships to generate positive consequences.

- *Can people of unequal status engage in truly caring relationships?*

There is evidence in the stories presented here that adults can and do have satisfactory, caring relationships with young people, despite the economic and status differences that sometimes exist between them. For example, Camblin and White (chapter 3) found that their sample of young African-American grandmothers show their caring for their daughters and grandchildren by tenaciously engaging in self-sacrifice in support of the family unit. In chapter 6, Smith observed that a day-care teacher in an urban high school went well beyond her official duties in caring for her students, including helping them with personal problems. On the other side, there are several stories in this volume that point to unsatisfactory, uncaring relationships between adults and young people. I say uncaring, despite the fact that some of the authors argue that these are caring relationships that simply lack a tenacious character. This distinction is artificial, I would argue, in that those who "care" feel obliged to maintain their sense of commitment over time. Milgram and Briton (chapter 4) identify four students who persevered in school, despite the lack of financial and/or emotional support from their parents. Hawkins (chapter 2) and Zorn (chapter 7) identify schools in which many of the staff do not care for students who deviate from the norms. Taking this varied evidence into consideration, it appears that children are regularly placed in contexts in which adults around them have little personal interest in their development into adults. This, I would argue, is not in itself evidence of the poor moral quality of adult citizens in the United States. In order to understand it, we must consider two separate dimensions of the problem: the mass nature of education and the labeling that occurs within schools.

It is a fact of modern life that we live in the immediate vicinity of countless others whom we do not know personally. Put another way, we live in a mass society (Mills, 1956, 1959). By its very nature, we are encouraged to perceive others as objects, not worthy of our individual attention. This principle is exemplified in a fictitious walk down a street in Manhattan, as opposed to "Smalltown, U.S.A." The first setting almost demands that you refrain from interacting with those around you. Failure to do so might reasonably be associated with the imposition of negative sanctions. The Smalltown setting almost demands the opposite; that is, the explicit recognition of many known individuals, on pain of punishment for failing to do so. This illustration is intended to demonstrate that context makes a difference in how we relate to others around us. Relationships emerge differently in mass contexts than in more intimate ones, and in roles where we request the followership of others than in ones where we are equal participants. So, too, does this principle apply to the relationship between teachers and students in schools. Some schools are integral parts of their communities. One might imagine that this occurs most often in places where the community is relatively homogeneous, and where teachers and administrators have grown up in that community or ones like it. In places such as these, it is easy to imagine teachers creating "webs of care" for their students, because they know them (or perhaps of them, or their families) from other contexts. They may be privy to peculiarities that help them to understand individual deviations from the norm. On the other hand, many schools in the United States resemble factories in their size, outward appearance, and in the relationships that develop within them. It is easy to see why some have called this mass education. It most closely resembles the processing of groups. Students in many schools spend their days with as many as eight different adults, in relatively short, 40-minute time segments. Teachers, conversely, often spend their days in front of six (or more) groups of 25 to 35 students, many of whom would rather be elsewhere. They must administer the distribution of a limited resource (i.e., grades) to students who theoretically engage each other in a competition that helps to determine their future status as adults in the community. This is not a structure that is conducive to the development of close, caring relationships between teachers and students. The finding that some individuals manage to create strong bonds with some students is remarkable, not the fact that these relationships are typically fraught with uncertainties (Lortie, 1975).

The literature on tracking and ability grouping within schools supports the generalization that schools are stratifying institutions (Oakes, 1985; Rist, 1970; Rosenbaum, 1976). Students are labeled and grouped according to predictions of their probable future place in the economy. Then they are segregated from others deemed to be unlike them in certain characteristics, creating a castelike order within schools that has the official endorsement of adults running those institutions. Despite attempts to disguise this reality, students generally know their place within the stratification system of the school. In addition, students recognize that marks represent adult evaluations of their academic ability and efforts. Although these systems of tracking and grading probably act to motivate those students in the top half of the class, I am doubtful that they have anything but detrimental effects on those in the bottom half. I argue that the above described system has the effect of dampening the latter group's participation in the learning process as it is defined by schools, affecting their relationships with teachers and other authorities. Subjectively understanding their low place in the system, these students simply have less vested interest in conforming to its demands.

Although adults and youth can engage in caring relationships, it appears that structural arrangements in schools help to make this a rarity. This is not a phenomenon to be understood on an individual level: Charismatic teachers with special talents should not be held up as role models, implying that there is something wrong with the majority of staffmembers. Most teachers are probably capable of caring about others, but less so in the contexts in which we ask them to work. When at-risk students consistently express the opinion that most of their teachers do not care about them or their personal development (Hamovitch, 1997), this is an epidemic, not just an illness. This suggests that solutions must involve a restructuring of factors that impinge on such relationships.

- *How does tenacious caring manifest itself in the real world? Is it a phenomenon with a diversity of appearances?*

It is my observation that tenacious caring is almost exclusively the domain of family. Because I have argued that the duration of a relationship is fundamental to tenacity, the issue of time needs to be explicitly addressed. Just how much time must be committed to caring for another for that relationship to be defined as tenacious? Obviously, there is no sensible answer to this question that speaks of minutes or hours or other finite units. However, there are fundamental differences between the concern that even "caring" adults dispense within their formal statuses in public institutions and those that are typical within a family (however defined). I feel differently about my own children than I do about my students. Generally, I operate under the assumption that my relations within the family are there for the long term, whereas those with students come and go. I know that caring involves entering the private domain of the other, and generally limit myself in my invasiveness. However, I define the private domain more expansively among my students than among my immediate family members. Asking a student a simple question like, "What did you do last night?" might be interpreted as an unwanted invasion of the private sphere (and yet be completely normative for another family member to ask). Thus, *tenacious caring* may be an inappropriate concept to help us idealize relations between students and teachers. Relations that occur within nonfamily institutions lack the longevity, the emotional commitment or intensity that is normative among family members (or perhaps between the closest of friends). I believe that holding tenacious caring out as a model applicable to the teacher student relationship distorts the nature of that association.

This is not to argue that caring (of the nontenacious variety) is not an important element in defining an ideal relationship between teachers and their students. It is just that when teachers care for their students, sometimes they act toward them in ways that the students themselves would not recognize as caring. Caring might also be invisible to the observer because it manifests itself in so many forms. The literature has restricted its definition of caring to include relational elements such as genuinely listening to the other and taking the other into account in one's actions (Noddings, 1992). But this is a limited understanding of caring. Caring also includes teachers who care enough to "push" their students toward excellence by demanding growth and development, and by having high expectations for students. It includes expending time and effort in thinking about curriculum matters and preparing classroom experiences for students. Another dimension of caring includes making careful judgments about what one communicates to students about their development via one's oral and written comments and the grades that one assigns. In short, it should be recognized that caring is a concept with dimensions beyond the relational. Right now, the caring literature implies that adults with authority over children are divided into two groups: those who are caring and uncaring in their relationships with their students. The relational definition of caring limits our thinking in this area, and unfairly labels many caring teachers as uncaring because it fails to closely inspect the motivations for behaviors that on the surface may appear to be neutral or even unsupporting of children.

- *Does caring have the power to help students overcome barriers that seem to be related to economic, racial, gender, and other barriers?*

The chapters in this volume either overlook this question or encourage the reader to hope that the answer to it is in the affirmative. The presented evidence, however, does not convince me that caring parents and school staff can, by themselves, make up for barriers to academic success that exist because of students' class, race, gender, and other statuses. My reading of chapter 3 for example, left me less hopeful than the researchers or Alisa's mother about Alisa's chances for future educational success. Cleo's hope for her daughter seemed almost desperate, making me wonder how likely it is that Alisa will ever graduate from high school. Mrs. Hurter (chapter 6) appears to be a gifted and sensitive day-care teacher in an inner-city high school, but I wonder about accepting at face value the inference that she can really make a difference in the life chances of her students and student parents. My own study of a caring after-school compensatory education program for at-risk youth (Hamovitch, 1997) shows that appearances can be deceptive. Despite the tenacious caring of the director and his staff, the students maintained a dismal school record. There were just too many factors in these students' lives that even a caring staff could not control for: unlawful or unruly behavior, pregnancy, a weak academic knowledge base, experiences of racism, a long-standing distrust of local schools, and so on. In short, there is evidence that relational caring is not enough to paper over huge crevices or fissures in many students' lives.

AN INFERENCE

The studies in this volume provide evidence that suggests that tenacious caring can sometimes be associated with positive and hopeful outcomes, albeit ones that encourage the kinds of conformity that adults desire. For example, Milgram and Briton (chapter 4) propose that some children have sufficient resources to be tenacious on their own behalf, and that self-caring can help individuals surmount obstacles. Hawkins (chapter 2) presents a case of a parent tenaciously and successfully lobbying the school on behalf of her son, who she fears is being pushed out by staff who blame the student for his deficiencies. Heydt (chapter 5) suggests that parents who tenaciously enforce rules about schoolwork can make a big difference in the likelihood that their children will experience academic success, even in adverse circumstances. Smith (chapter 6) suggests that high school-aged parents should be listened to sympathetically, without the arrogance that sometimes accompanies middle-class caregivers' relationships with lower class clients. She argues that tenaciously caring relationships within a school context can help students respond resourcefully to very difficult circumstances. Zorn (chapter 7) suggests that tenaciously caring teachers can make a difference in the academic success of their students. She uses the vivid metaphor *web of care* to describe the situation of some students who are surrounded by adults who take a tenacious interest in their progress. Finally, Huston (chapter 8) suggests that we can create genuinely caring high schools, based on important principles such as small size, individualized learning, and the availability of social and psychological services.

Do people care enough to push institutions in directions that they think are positive for others whose voices are rarely listened to? Do those at risk themselves know how to push institutions in directions that would benefit them? Encouraging institutions to change long-established routines and practices is perilous work, in which one is likely to suffer the wrath of those whose interests and perspectives do not coincide with your own. The fact that a literature has sprung up exploring the plight of the disenfranchised in the hands of uncaring adults is evidence that people are looking for explanations of and solutions for situations that are unjust. I am suggesting that more useful answers are to be found in looking at issues of power and its distribution among different groups in our society as a whole.

As I see it, those who care about at-risk students have an obligation to demonstrate their caring by looking beyond seeking ways to incrementally improve relations within existing structures. Caring advocates should use that concern as a springboard to change structures and practices that make many students at-risk in the first place (and thus thought to be in special need of caring). Thus, the concept of *caring* should be integrated into researchers' explorations of other factors associated with at-risk status, and should be considered in proposals for change.

10

Postscript

Mary Anne Pitman
University of Cincinnati
Debbie Zorn
University of Cincinnati

We have been very informed by this process, and we hope that others seeking to understand and improve the lives of urban youth can use these stories to further their work. We do believe that *tenacity* is an important concept that extends the caring paradigm beyond constancy and continuation, and, at the same time, problematizes the notion that the institution of schooling is amenable to fostering caring relationships beyond its own inward workings.

We learned that urban youth burdened by racism, but not poverty, can survive the structures of urban schooling in order to graduate with a financially and educationally usable credential—if a parent (see Hawkins, chapter 2) pays attention the whole way through, intervening at every turn and insisting that the structure of schooling admit into its processes the "involvement" of a parent. But when poverty is added to racism, as it was in the lives of the young grandmothers (Camblin & White, chapter 3), the attentiveness may not be enough to ensure success. Because "urban" here implies chaotic social and economic structures (Smith, chapter 6; Zorn, chapter 7; Huston, chapter 8), families as war zones (Heydt, chapter 5) and lost children (Milgram & Briton, chapter 4), we have asked, can those children have orderly lives that include a rhythm of schooling? Our answer is, we don't think so—UNLESS, there is a tenacious relationship that insists on making it so.

Our examples of tenacity within school settings (see chapters 6, 7, and 8) are indeed extraordinary circumstances—found within special interventions that of necessity change some of the structural arrangements of schooling (e.g., smaller class sizes, reduced teaching loads) to enable personnel to offer increased attention to students (not unlike the arrangements that are more common to special education, early childhood education, and the enriched activities and settings that are most accessible to unalienated middle-class students). These unusual circumstances, nevertheless, are still pockets within a largely impersonal institutional context.

The form of story was chosen for this volume for its ability to privilege "feelings, purposes, images, aspirations, and personal meanings" (Carter, 1993, p. 7). If, as Noddings (1991) suggested "stories have the power to direct and change our lives" (p. 157), then these isolated examples of individual change are offered as hope for the merest possibility of social change. We agree with Hamovitch (chapter 9) that school survival for urban children is a topic of much concern precisely because of unchanging social, including political and economic, and institutional structural conditions. If structural changes were realistically in place anywhere, then school survival for urban children would not be an urgent and alarming issue. It is precisely because of the structure of urban schooling as it has existed in the 1990s that we forefront the complexity of tenacious human agency. Except for Kent (chapter 8), the schools themselves and the stories we tell of their students are not conducive to retention, to being able to hang on and stay there, much less succeed, without the tenacious attention of relationships, or, alternatively, the schools' tenacious neutrality in the face of chaos (see chapter 5).

As these stories attest, caring overtures, when instituted piecemeal and sporadically within schools, are received with skepticism and resisted by students who have been placed at-risk for school success by society and institution. Successful tenacious, trusting relationships are not the norm, even under the most ideal circumstances. Most professionals in education are scarcely prepared to exercise skills that require negotiating cultural and class boundaries as well as unequal power relationships. Successfully meeting the curriculum and instructional needs of these students requires another stretch that, we would argue, cannot be divorced from, but grows out of relational understanding and trust. We do not, however, suggest that teachers should be more caring, as though caring, as suggested by some of the current literature, were some kind of simple change in pedagogy that once recognized could be used by any competent teacher. Still, our data shows that caring—if it occurs in the form of a tenacious relationship—can provide a safety net.

We offer tenacious caring, therefore, as a small piece of the overall puzzle of how to meet the pressing educational needs of urban secondary school students—not as a panacea, and certainly not as a solution that can stand by itself. In the institutional and noninstitutional settings where we found it, the obstacles to success of any kind for these students continue to be legion. In most secondary school settings there exist nearly unsurmountable structural and cultural barriers to school personnel being able to develop any sort of caring, let alone tenaciously caring relationships with students. It is not that urban high school teachers are uncaring, but that the system generally dictates against their being able to act on that care in any meaningful terms.

So, while schools are necessarily preoccupied by the need to try to address both the immediate demands of providing safe environments and crowd control in overcrowded understaffed buildings, and the political and societal demands for academic monitoring in the form of proficiency testing, enforcement of drug laws, and myriad other similar demands placed on the young by the mature, there is little wonder that a large percentage of urban adolescents give up on school attendance. They subsequently lose out on, or are closed out of access to higher education and/or employment. In the meantime, while we wait for change and work for change to come to urban institutions that serve the young, we can attend to the needs of one young person and hang on, refusing to go away or give up, refusing to mind our own business, insisting on caring about, being there, and again.

References

Anyon, J. (1981). Social class and school knowledge. *Curriculum Inquiry, 1*(1), 342.

Au, K., & Kawakami, A. J. (1991). Culture and ownership: Schooling of minority students. *Childhood Education, 67*(5), 280-284.

Au, K., & Mason, J. M. (1983). Cultural congruence in classroom participation structures: Achieving a balance of rights. *Discourse Processes, 6,* 145-167.

Bernard, J. (1974). *The future of motherhood.* New York: Penguin Books.

Bernstein, B. (1977). Social class, language and socialization. In J. Karabel & A. H. Halsey (Eds.), *Power and ideology in education* (pp. 473-486). New York: Oxford University Press.

Bourdieu, P. (1977). Cultural reproduction and social reproduction. In J. Karabel & A. H. Halsey (Eds.), *Power and ideology in education* (pp. 487-511). New York: Oxford University Press.

Bowles, S., & Gintis, H. (1976). *Schooling in capitalist America.* New York: Basic Books.

Brown, L. M., & Gilligan, C. (1992). *Meeting at the crossroads: Women's psychology and girls' development.* Cambridge, MA: Harvard University Press.

Buber, M. (1965). *Between man and man.* New York: Macmillan

Callahan, R. E. (1962). *Education and the cult of efficiency.* Chicago: University of Chicago Press.

Carter, K. (1993). The place of story in the study of teaching and teacher education. *Educational Researcher, 22*(1), 5-12.

Casey, K. (1995). The new narrative research in education. *Review of Research in Education, 21,* 211-253.

Chaskin, R. J., & Rauner, D. M. (1995). Youth and caring: An introduction. *Phi Delta Kappan, 76,* 667-674.

Chodorow, N. (1978). *The reproduction of mothering.* Berkeley: University of California Press.

Coleman, J., Campbell, E., Hobson, C., McPartland, J., Mood, A., Weinfeld, F., & York, R. (1966). *Equality of educational opportunity*. Washington, DC: U.S. Office of Education.

Cornbleth, C. (1990). *Curriculum in context*. London: Falmer Press.

Cusick, P. A. (1973). *Inside high school: The students' world*. New York: Holt, Rinehart & Winston.

Eaker-Rich, D., & Van Galen, J. (Eds.). (1996). *Caring in an unjust world*. Albany: State University of New York Press.

Eaker-Rich, D., Van Galen, J. A., & Timothy, E. L. (1996). Conclusion. In D. Eaker-Rich & J. Van Galen (Eds.), *Caring in an unjust world* (pp. 231-237). Albany: State University of New York Press.

Fordham, S. (1991). Peer-proofing academic competition among black adolescents: "Acting White" Black American style. In C. Sleeter (Ed.), *Empowerment through multicultural education* Albany: State University of New York Press.

Forrest, J., & Singh, S. (1990). The sexual and reproductive behavior of American women, 1982-1988. *Family Planning Perspectives, 22,* 206-215.

Freire, P. (1970). *Pedagogy of the oppressed*. New York: Herder and Herder.

Freire, P. (1973). *Education for critical consciousness*. New York: Continuum.

Furstenburg, F., & Crawford, A. (1978). Family support: Helping teenage mothers to cope. *Family Planning Perspectives, 10,* 322-333.

Furstenburg, F., Levine, J., & Brooks-Gunn, J. (1990). The children of teenage mothers: Patterns of early childbearing in two generations. *Family Planning Perspectives, 22,* 54-61.

Garcia-Coll, C., Hoffman, C., & Oh, W. (1987). The social ecology and early parenting of Caucasian adolescent mothers. *Child Development, 58,* 955-963.

Gibson, R. (1986). *Critical theory and education*. London: Hodder & Stroughton.

Gilligan, C. (1982). *In a different voice*. Cambridge, MA: Harvard University Press.

Gormley, A., & Brodzinsky, D. (1993). *Lifespan human development* (5th ed.). Fort Worth, TX: Harcourt Brace Jovanovich College Publishers.

Hamovitch, B. A. (1995). Caring in an institutional context: Can it really occur? *Educational Foundations, 9*(4), 25-39.

Hamovitch, B. A. (1997). *Staying after school: At-risk students in a compensatory education program*. Westport, CT: Praeger.

Harris, C., Pitman, M.A., Hensley, B., & Zorn, D. (1997). *A cross cultural study of gender and knowledge: Telling the extraordinary stories of ordinary women's lives*. Unpublished manuscript, University of Cincinnati, Cincinnati, OH.

Heiddeger, M. (1962). *Being and time*. New York: Harper & Row. (Original work published 1927)

Heydt, M. J. (1994). *In their own words: A qualitative study of growing up with chemical dependency and sexual child abuse.* Unpublished doctoral dissertation, University of Cincinnati, Cincinnati, OH.

hooks, b. (1994). *Teaching to transgress: Education as the practice of freedom.* New York: Routledge.

Jencks, C., Smith, M., Acland, H., Bane, M., Cohen, D., Gintis, H., Heyns, B., & Michelson, S. (1972). *Inequality: A reassessment of the effect of family and schooling in America.* New York: Basic Books.

Kivett, V. (1993). Racial comparisons of the grandmother's role: Implications for strengthening the family support system of older black women. *Family Relations, 45,* 165-172.

Kuhn, T. (1962). *The structure of scientific revolutions.* Chicago: University of Chicago Press.

Lortie, D. C. (1975). *Schoolteacher: A sociological study.* Chicago: University of Chicago Press.

Martin, J. R. (1992). *The schoolhome: Rethinking schools for changing families.* Cambridge, MA: Harvard University Press.

Matthews, S., & Sprey J. (1985). Adolescents' relationships with grandparents. *Journal of Gerontology, 40,* 621-626.

McGee, E. (1982). *Too little, too late.* New York: Ford Foundation.

Meier, D. (1998). Can the odds be changed? *Phi Delta Kappan, 79*(5), 358-362.

Miller, G. (1991). *Enforcing the work ethic: Rhetoric and everyday life in a work incentive program.* Albany: State University of New York Press.

Mills, C. W. (1956). *The power elite.* New York: Oxford University Press.

Mills, C. W. (1959). *The sociological imagination.* New York: Oxford University Press.

Montague, A. (1970). *The direction of human development.* New York: Holt, Rinehart & Winston.

Noblit, G. W. (1993a). Power and caring. *American Educational Research Journal, 30*(1), 23-38.

Noblit, G. W. (1993b). Review of "The challenge to care in schools: An alternative approach to education." *Educational Studies, 24*(4), 369-372.

Noddings, N. (1984). *Caring: A feminine approach to ethics and moral education.* Berkeley: University of California Press.

Noddings, N. (1988). An ethic of caring and its implications for instructional arrangements. *American Journal of Education, 96*(2), 215-230.

Noddings, N. (1992). *The challenge to care in schools: An alternative approach to education.* New York: Teachers College Press.

Noddings, N. (1995). Teaching themes of care. *Phi Delta Kappan, 76,* 675-679.

Oakes, J. (1985). *Keeping track: How schools structure inequality.* Binghamton, NY: Vail-Ballou Press.

Ogbu, J. (1974). *The next generation: An ethnography of education in an urban neighborhood.* New York: Academic Press.

Ogbu, J. (1978). *Minority education and caste: The American system in cross-cultural perspective.* New York: Academic Press.

Osofsky, J., & Osofsky H. (1978). Teenage pregnancy: Psychological considerations. *Clinical Obstetrics and Gynecology, 21,* 1161-1173.

Page, R. (1991). *Lower-track classrooms: A curricular and cultural perspective.* New York: Teachers College Press.

The Personal Narratives Group. (1989). *Interpreting women's lives: Feminist theory and personal narratives.* Bloomington: Indiana University Press.

Pitman, M. A., Eisikovits, R. A., & Dobbert, M. L. (1989) *Culture acquisition: A holistic approach to human learning.* New York: Praeger.

Pitman, M. A., & Samuels, L. (1991, November). *Project HOPE: A qualitative evaluation of a school support program.* Paper presented at the annual meeting of the American Anthropological Association, Chicago, IL.

Prilliman, R., Eaker, D., & Kendrick, D. M. (Eds.). (1994). *The tapestry of caring: Education as nurturance.* Norwood, NJ: Ablex.

Polakow, V. (1993). *Lives on the edge: Single mothers and their children in the other America.* Chicago: University of Chicago Press.

Rist, R. (1970). Student social class and teacher expectations: The self-fulfilling prophecy of ghetto education. *Harvard Educational Review, 40,* 411-451.

Rosenbaum, J. E. (1976). *Making inequality: The hidden curriculum of high school tracking.* New York:Wiley.

Smith, M. L. (1990). *Walking the edges: Tracing literacy across three generations.* Unpublished doctoral dissertation, University of Cincinnati, Cincinnati, OH.

Smith, M. L. (1991). Cubbies, coloring, and computers: Learning to do school in a day care program. *Childhood Education, 67*(5), 317-318.

Smith, M. L. (1993). *Learning culture: Learning to do school.* Paper presented at the annual meeting of the American Anthropological Association, Washington, DC.

Solomon, R. P. (1989). Dropping out of academics. In L. Weis, E. Farrar, & H. G. Petrie (Eds.), *Dropouts from school: Issues, dilemmas & solutions* (pp. 51–84). Albany: State University of New York Press.

Swadener, B. B., & Lubeck, S. (Eds.). (1995). *Children and families "at promise": Deconstructing the discourse of risk.* Albany: State University of New York Press.

Usdansky, M. (1993, May 14). Teen mothers trip up a trend. *USA Today,* p. 7A.

Van Galen, J. A. (1996). Caring in community: The limitations of compassion in facilitating diversity. In D. Eaker-Rich & J. Van Galen (Eds.), *Caring in an unjust world.* Albany: State University of New York Press.

Van Galen, J., & Pitman, M. A. (Eds.). (1991). *Homeschooling: Political, historical and pedagogical perspectives.* Norwood, NJ: Ablex.

VanMaanan, J. (1988). *Tales of the field: On writing ethnography.* Chicago: University of Chicago Press.

Wehlage, G. G., Rutter, R. A., Smith, G. A., Lesko, N., & Fernandez, R. R. (1989). *Reducing the risk: Schools and communities of support.* London & New York: Falmer Press.

Weis, L. (1985). *Between two worlds: Black students in an urban community college.* Boston: Routledge & Kegan Paul.

Witherall, C., & Noddings, N. (Eds.). (1991). *Stories lives tell: Narrative and dialogue in education.* New York: Teachers College Press.

Woods, P. (1990). *The happiest days?: How pupils cope with school.* London & Philadelphia: Falmer Press.

Author Index

Subject Index